Y0-CXR-124

the enlightened

A SANBENITO
(*After* Picart)

the enlightened

THE WRITINGS OF
LUIS DE CARVAJAL, EL MOZO

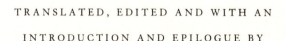

TRANSLATED, EDITED AND WITH AN
INTRODUCTION AND EPILOGUE BY

SEYMOUR B. LIEBMAN

PREFACE BY ALLAN NEVINS

UNIVERSITY OF MIAMI PRESS
Coral Gables, Florida

LIBRARY

JAN 18 1968

UNIVERSITY OF THE PACIFIC

177440

Copyright © 1967 by
UNIVERSITY OF MIAMI PRESS

Library of Congress Catalog Card No. 67–28272

Designed by Harvey Satenstein

MANUFACTURED IN THE UNITED STATES OF AMERICA

IN MEMORY

OF

Luis de Carvajal, *el Mozo*
WHO DIED FOR THE SAKE OF THE HOLY NAME

preface

 AMONG THE DOCUMENTS illustrating the life of the early European settlers on the North American continent those preserved by the Mexican Inquisition exercise a special fascination. Here we learn about the travails of persons who tried to escape religious persecution in their home country as did later the Pilgrim Fathers reaching Massachusetts Bay. Unlike the English refugees, however, these Spanish colonists were not allowed to leave Spain if they were descendants of Jews, Moors, or "heretics," while after arriving in the New World they often fell into the hands of the ruthless agents of the Inquisition and suffered death by burning.

One of the most remarkable martyrs of this kind was Luis de Carvajal, *el Mozo* (the Younger) who, although the nephew of an influential admiral and governor, was ultimately executed by the Inquisition in 1596. A thinker and poet of merit, Carvajal left behind a number of writings of both religious and human interest which belong to the most noteworthy documents extant from sixteenth-century Mexico. These are presented here in an accurate English translation with an illuminating introduction and well-informed notes by Professor Seymour B. Liebman. They should prove of considerable interest not only to scholars but also to general readers attracted to the story of the early beginnings of European civilization in the Americas, as well as of the heroic vicissitudes of memorable religious martyrs.

ALLAN NEVINS

fOREWORD

―――――――•◆•―――――――

THE ONLY KNOWN extant writings by a Jew in Mexico during the Spanish colonial period, 1521–1821, are the memoirs, letters, and will written during 1595 and 1596 by Luis de Carvajal, *el Mozo* (the Younger). During this period, branches of the Spanish Inquisition were established in all the Spanish possessions of the New World. The Inquisition was actively engaged in ferreting out heresy, and among its victims were secret, or crypto-Jews.

Carvajal's writings reveal the thoughts and emotions of the young man toward the Inquisition and the inquisitors. They also portray his family relationships, religious activities, and various facets of the social and economic life of the colony at the end of the sixteenth century. For these reasons and because they are the earliest known writings by Iberian Jews in the New World, their publication in English is important.

These works transcend the significance of the lives of the individuals involved. The observation of Allan Nevins that the Bible is local, individual history "writ large," overshadowing the great personalities and their eminent contributions, is applicable to the contents of the manuscripts preserved for posterity in the files and documents of the Mexican Inquisition.

While a considerable amount has been written in Spanish about Luis de Carvajal the Younger, historians and others have erred in recording one or more details of his life and of the lives of his family. It is regrettable that most authors have copied what others have written and that none except Alfonso Toro has incorporated in his work any part of Luis' *Memorias* (Memoirs, or autobiography), letters, or last will and testament. History does not repeat itself so much as historians repeat each other's errors. A wealth of material pertaining to the Carvajal family in the Inquisition Section of the Mexican National Archives is available to all. However, some of this material was stolen from the Archives in 1932 and at other times. Fortunately, part of the stolen material had previously been copied and later was published by Luis González Obregón and Alfonso Toro. The exact transcription of the manuscripts by Luis González Obregón appears in the *Procesos de Luis de Carvajal* (*el Mozo*), Publications del Archivo General de la Nación, Vol. XXVIII (Mexico City, 1935). The *Procesos* include the memoirs, letters, and last will and testament of Luis de Carvajal, and the translations that follow here are based on that volume. Alfonso Toro included his transcription of the memoirs as an appendix to his *La Familia Carvajal,* 2 vols. (Mexico City, 1944), pages 315–339.

There are other original Inquisition documents pertaining to the Carvajal family in the Henry E. Huntington Library at San Marino, California, and elsewhere. The procesos (trial proceedings) of Luis' niece, Leonor de Cáceres, at the Huntington Library yield much important data on the compositions of young Luis and on the lives of the young girl and her mother, Luis' sister Catalina.

The preserved writings of Luis do not give a full picture of the young Spanish Jew, nor is the introduction which precedes this translation intended to give a full biographical sketch. Such an account would require a book in itself. The record of Luis' two trials before the Mexican Inquisition comprises over four hundred printed pages. To learn the meaningful minutiae of his life and all important details and to secure that well-rounded picture which every biographer desires to present, it would be necessary to digest and comment on the testimony adduced in the trial proceedings of many others who were his contemporaries. While the testimony of his uncle, Luis de Carvajal y de la Cueva, Governor of the New Kingdom of León, adds little, that of young Luis' sisters Isabel, Catalina, and Leonor, and of his friends Justa Méndez and Manuel de Lucena, adds much—in fact, practically every one of the forty-five Jews who were participants in the December 8, 1596 auto-da-fé (*auto de fé* in Spanish) referred to incidents in the life of Luis and to his religious practices.

I wish to thank Miss Haydée Noya of the Huntington Library for her cooperation in supplying data on the material in the Douglas Collection at the Library, which led to my research there, and for her aid and suggestions in the problems of translation. Thanks are due to *Judaism* for relinquishing my translation in manuscript of the last will and testament, which had been accepted for publication .by that periodical.

The encouragement of Allan Nevins toward publication of this material as a book rather than as a monograph has resulted in the use of further background material and an Epilogue, all of which extend the story of the Carvajal family to more than a century after the demise of the principal figure.

My devoted wife, Malvina W. Liebman, and Mrs. Alice Keesling aided in the translation of some of the liturgical verses. Sra. Yolanda Snaiderman and Sra. Carmen Rivas helped with the original translation of parts of the documents. Luis A. Peinado, S.J., checked some of the more problematic Latin citations. Thanks are extended to the staff of the Huntington Library for valuable assistance in reading the manuscript, suggesting editorial changes, and checking Latin translations.

Special acknowledgment for the selection of the pictorial material is due Samuel S. Matza, Librarian in the Jewish Division of the New York Public Library who helped Harvey Satenstein, our distinguished designer, in his initial typographic planning. This book took added meaning to all concerned and in so doing, has helped make my efforts to illuminate the immortal message of Luis de Carvajal, *el Mozo* brighter.

The final version is, however, my sole responsibility. In some instances I have heeded an old rabbinic precept on translations that one must sometimes be a traitor to the original in order to convey the ideas and spirit of a document in another language.

Luis' Latin citations, which are usually biblical quotations, have been retained exactly as they appear in the González Obregón transcription of the original documents. Some of the citations have come down to us in a fragmentary, abbreviated, or corrupt form. It must be kept in mind that Luis was writing from memory and had inadequate writing materials. Some of the obvious errors may have crept in during the transcription of the documents from their original source. Where the Latin from which Luis is quoting can easily be identified, the footnotes show the source.

[11]

In the case of biblical quotations from the vernacular, Luis' citations are not always exact or complete. An additional reason for variance here is that Luis may have relied on the translations of his fellow Jew, Manuel de Morales, which were made from an unknown source. Direct biblical quotations in the vernacular also have been identified in the footnotes when their source can be suggested. Quotations from the Vulgate and Douay Version are identified as Vulg. and D.V. Some quotations follow the Jewish Publication Society translation, the Authorized Version (*The Holy Scriptures According to the Masoretic Text,* Philadelphia, 1917) and are identified as JPS. I have also relied upon the Revised Version (Oxford, 1885), identified as R.V., as used by Chief Rabbi J. F. Hertz in his *The Pentateuch and Haftorahs* (London, 1936).

This book is dedicated to the author of the works that are translated in the pages that follow. The life, the thoughts, and the spirit of a young man who would have been immortalized had he lived in any other time or place deserve to be recalled from obscurity.

S.B.L.

Miami, Florida
November, 1967

contents

ILLUSTRATIONS

the enlightened

FIG. 1: Title page of the rules and regulations for officials
of the Holy Office of the Mexican Inquisition

introduction

IN RABBINIC LITERATURE there is a statement that a man acquires three names during his lifetime: the first is given to him by his parents at birth; the second is the name by which he is known among his intimates as he approaches maturity; the third is the epitaph which should be placed on his tombstone after his death. This last epitomizes what his life represented and what people thought of him.

Luis de Carvajal, *el Mozo* (the Younger) was named Luis Rodríguez de Carvajal at birth. As a result of a vision he had when imprisoned in the Inquisition secret cells he adopted the name Joseph Lumbroso (the Enlightened); this name was appended to his Memoirs and his last will and testament. On December 8, 1596, Luis was burned at the stake in an auto-da-fé in Mexico City, after having been tried by the Tribunal of the Holy Office of the Inquisition, having been found guilty of being a Jew, and of having observed Jewish religious practices. Luis' epitaph was written by a Dominican monk, Fray Alonso de Contreras, who spent the last hours of the young man's life with him. In his *Relación* (final report to the inquisitors), Fray Alonso wrote:

"He was always such a good Jew and reconciled his understanding, which was very profound and sensitive, with the divine determination with which he was highly inspired, to defend the law of God and to fight for it. I have no doubt that if he had lived before the Incarnation of our Redeemer, he would have been a heroic Hebrew, and today his name would be as famous in the Bible

[19]

as are the names of those who died in defense of their law when it was necessary."[1]

When Hernán Cortés completed the conquest of Mexico on August 13, 1521, there were Jews in his company. Other Jews arrived later in spite of decrees barring the Spanish colonies in the New World to Jews, Moors, and other heretics, and to their descendants to the fourth generation. Licenses to emigrate to the New World were issued only to Spanish Catholics. Jews and others paid bribes, forged papers, and appropriated old Catholic names from tombstones in Spain in their efforts to emigrate. Their love of Spain, Spanish customs, and the Spanish language was as strong as their devotion to their forbidden faith. They sought to live in a Spanish environment despite the dangers involved in exposure to the activities of the Inquisition.

Two Jews were burned at the stake in Mexico City in 1528.[2] Two others were accused, found guilty, and reconciled. The Jews who came to the shores of New Spain prior to 1580 were converts to Catholicism or descendants of converts. They were known as *nuevo-cristianos* (New Christians), *hebreo-cristianos* (Hebrew Christians), *conversos* (converts), or *judaizantes* (practitioners of Jewish rites, sometimes also used as a synonym for *judíos,* Jews). They are more correctly termed *crypto-judíos* (secret Jews). To the best of this writer's knowledge the word *marrano* (swine) was never used by any of the five Inquisition tribunals in the Spanish dependencies. Alfonso Toro wrote that *marrano* was used by Jews to describe other Jews who had sincerely embraced Christianity. However, many writers use the word as a synonym for crypto-Jew and do not distinguish between those who had been baptized and those who had not been but who nevertheless practiced Judaism sub rosa to avoid entanglements with the Spanish authorities.

The Jews of the era extending from 1521 to 1580 in New Spain were not noted for their learning or devout religious observances. Their loyalty to the faith of their forefathers is partially explained by the

1. "Ultimos momentos y conversión de Luis de Carvajal, 1596," *Anales de Museo Nacional de Arqueología* III (1925), pp. 64–78, contains a transcription of the report of Fray Alonso de Contreras. The material quoted here appears on pp. 64–65.
2. Seymour B. Liebman, "Hernando Alonso: The First Jew on the North American Continent," *Journal of Inter-American Studies,* V (1963), p. 291.

biblical expression applied to the early Jews, "a stiff-necked people," and by their Spanish psyche, which was dominated by ambivalence and individualism.

Approximately one hundred thousand Jews found refuge in Portugal after Ferdinand's and Isabella's Decree of Expulsion in 1492. In 1497 Portugal decreed the expulsion of Jews. There were great pogroms in Lisbon, Coimbra, and other Portuguese cities during the first decade of the sixteenth century, but the Jews in the hinterlands found comparative safety. In Lisbon and other places children were sometimes torn from the arms of their parents and dragged to the baptismal font.

In 1579 the Portuguese royal dynasty ended for lack of an heir, and Spain annexed the Lusitanian nation with ease. The annexation filled the Jews of Portugal with great consternation. They knew that the Spanish Inquisition would supersede the Portuguese Inquisition, which had never been as active as that of Spain. With this in mind, many Jews fled to the New World, using the various available means of deception to get into the country. The forty-five Jews in the auto-da-fé of December 8, 1596 in Mexico City exceeded in number the twenty-three who landed in New Amsterdam in 1654. One hundred and twenty-three other Jews in Mexico were implicated by Luis alone during his second trial from February, 1595 to December, 1596.

By 1590 a Jewish community was well established in Mexico City. The Tribunal of the Holy Office was established in 1571 and took over from bishops and others those inquisitorial functions that they had theretofore exercised under their episcopal powers. Among the heretics imprisoned, tried, and either reconciled or executed were those Jews accused, as the decrees usually stated, of having followed the dead law of Moses. Those who recanted and were thought to be truly *reconciliado* (reconciled to the Church) were allowed to leave the *Casa de la Inquisición* (the House of Inquisition, which is still standing in Mexico City), under various degrees of surveillance. Many were required to wear the *sanbenito* (or *sambenito*), a penitential garment which was worn over the penitent's other clothing. It was of coarse material and looked like a burlap bag. A cross and figures were painted on it to signify the nature of the sin for which penance was being done. The period for which the garment was to be worn varied from six months to several years. After the penance was completed, the garment was hung on the Cathedral wall in Mexico City, and the name of the

Fig. 2: An eighteenth century artist's conception of penitents wearing sanbenitos that indicate various infractions against Catholic law. The three on the left signify minor offenses; the three on the right with mitres (*corozas*) denote major violations (heresy, bigamy, perjury, etc.). The figure on the extreme right has been condemned to the stake.

penitent and other data were painted on it. Ultimately, because of lack of space, *tabillas,* small strips of cloth, were substituted for the sanbenitos.

Portuguese Jews had retained the principles and tenets of their religion to a greater extent than had their Spanish coreligionists. Their practices were more complete and their learning less superficial. In Portugal they had among themselves more spiritual leaders than in Spain, and Portuguese Jewry had retained greater contacts with other Jewish communities. In Lisbon there was a Grand Rabbi who was apprehended by the Inquisition about 1560 and burned at the stake. His son-in-law, Licenciado (Dr.) Manuel de Morales, a physician known among the Jews as Abraham de Morales, was a very learned Jew who emigrated to New Spain about 1580. He brought with him a book of prayers to which he added other supplications that he composed. He also translated Deuteronomy from Latin into the Spanish vernacular. The presence of men such as he in New Spain was significant because of the learning they disseminated and the inspiration for the continuing survival of Judaism they inculcated among youth. Among the disciples of Manuel de Morales was Luis de Carvajal, the Younger.

Luis de Carvajal, the Younger, was born in Benavente, Castile, about 1567. His name at birth was Luis Rodríguez de Carvajal. His father, Francisco Rodríguez de Matos, had been raised by the Count of Benavente. His mother, Francisca Núñez de Carvajal, was usually referred to as Francisca de Carvajal. Luis was one of nine living children. His elder brothers were Gaspar, who became a Dominican friar, and Baltasar; his elder sisters were Isabel, a childless widow, and Catalina, the mother of Leonor de Cáceres. Luis' younger brother was Miguel or Miguelito, born about 1576; and his younger sisters were Leonor, born about 1574, Mariana, born about 1577, and Ana or Anica, born about 1581.

In 1580 all the members of the family except the father dropped "Rodríguez" from their name, and all except Catalina substituted "Carvajal." They were then under the aegis of Luis de Carvajal y de la Cueva, brother of Francisca de Carvajal and the uncle of her children. Catalina took the name Catalina de la Cueva. The adoption of the patronymic of an illustrious relative was a common Spanish custom in

Table 1
GENEALOGICAL TABLE OF GOVERNOR LUIS DE CARVAJAL AND HIS SISTER,
FRANCISCA NÚÑEZ DE CARVAJAL, THE MOTHER OF
LUIS DE CARVAJAL, EL MOZO

Paternal

Maternal

Gutierre Vásquez de la Cueva = **Francisca de Carvajal**
f/Sayago, near Zamorra

Antonio de León = **Francisca Núñez**
f/Mogodorio · f/Mogodorio

Melchior Vásquez
f/Mirandela

Juan de Carvajal
f/Mogodorio;
a man-at-arms

Gaspar de Carvajal
f/Mogodorio
to Benavente

Catalina de León = **Jorge de León**
f/Mogodorio · farmer between Mirandela and Mogodorio

Antonio de León de León
broker for King of Portugal in Guinea

Duarte Alvaro de León
f/Medine del Campo

Isabel = **Enrique Pimentel**
Núñez · f/Mirandela

Francisco Jorge de Andrade
Captain General of port, dealer in Negro slaves; later an Augustinian monk in Mexico

Miguel = **Blanca Núñez Rodriguez**
f/Santo Domingo, broker of slaves for King of Portugal in Santo Domingo · f/Seville

Antonio de Carvajal
d. Oaxaca

Domingo de Carvajal
Jesuit in Medina del Campo

Francisca Núñez de Carvajal
b. 1546

= **Francisco Rodríguez de Matos**

Luis de Carvajal de la Cueva
b. 1540
d. 1590

= **Guiomar de Rivera**
f/Lisbon

see table 2 for continuation

b = approx. date of birth
d = approx. date of death
* = practicing Jew, where known
f/ = birthplace or residence

Table 2
GENEALOGICAL TABLE OF FAMILY OF LUIS DE CARVAJAL, EL MOZO

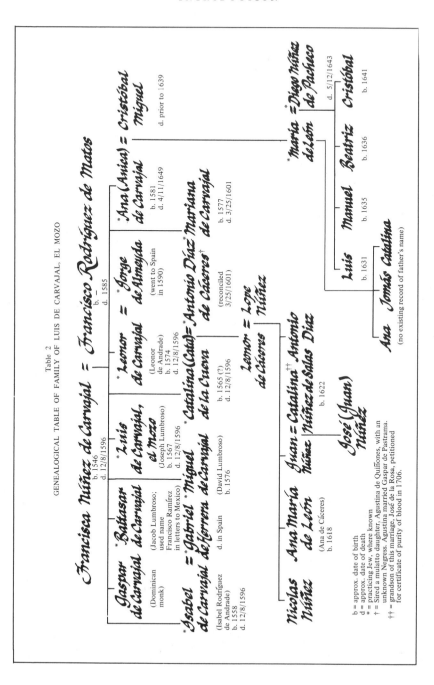

b = approx. date of birth
d = approx. date of death
* = practicing Jew, where known
† = Sired a mulatto daughter, Agustina de Quiñones, with an
unknown Negress. Agustina married Gaspar de Pastrana.
†† = grandson of this marriage, José de la Rosa, petitioned
for certificate of purity of blood in 1706.

the sixteenth century. Isabel de Carvajal was sometimes also known as Isabel Rodríguez de Arnade after another uncle.

Luis' uncle, the then-famed Luis de Carvajal, *el Conquistador,* held the title of admiral, having defeated the English in a naval encounter off the coast of New Spain in 1568. In the colonial period, "Mexico" meant only Mexico City. The colony was named Nueva España, New Spain, and its area included what is now the southwestern United States, Central America except for Panama, and the Philippine Islands. In 1579 Luis' uncle had received a royal contract from Philip II, awarding him the governorship of a newly created province, the New Kingdom of León, in the viceroyalty of New Spain. The New Kingdom of León extended from Tampico in modern Mexico to San Antonio, Texas, and ranged six hundred miles inland from the Gulf of Mexico. The governor and his entourage arrived in the Tampico area in 1580 and began colonization near the banks of the Panuco River.

The governor had coerced his brother-in-law, Francisco Rodríguez de Matos, to join him in coming to the New World instead of going to France by naming young Luis his heir and successor. The governor had no children, and his wife had refused to join his expedition. She, Doña Guiomar, was a crypto-Jewess but her husband never knew this. However, her niece Isabel knew her aunt's faith.

While the father of Luis de Carvajal, the Younger was born a full Jew, Luis' mother was of Jewish descent only on her maternal side. She had been betrothed when she was twelve years old, having been reared by an aunt who, it is presumed, was a secret Jewess. Francisca de Carvajal devoutly followed her husband's religion. Young Luis received a formal education in a Jesuit school from the time he was eleven until he was fourteen years of age. He could read and write Latin and Spanish and was well versed in mathematics, grammar, and rhetoric.

After the Decree of 1492 expelling the Jews from Spain, many of those who had been allowed to remain by converting to Catholicism retained secret allegiance to Judaism. These people, crypto-Jews, told their children of their Jewish ancestry when they were considered sufficiently mature to be entrusted with the secret. The practice of sending one child (usually the eldest) into the Church without informing him of his family's secert observances was often done to avert suspicion.

Exactly when Luis' father informed him that he was a Jew and that

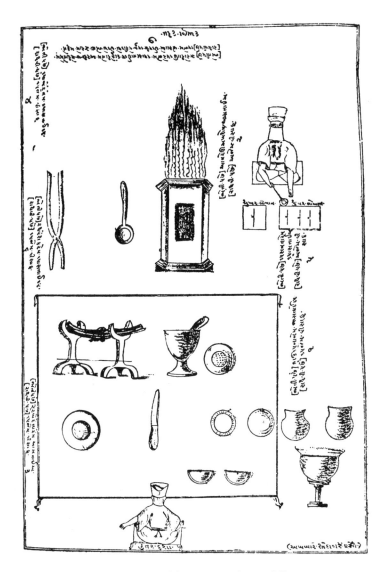

FIG. 3: Utensils used by Jews in the Middle Ages
(after Alfonso Toro)

he was to follow the Mosaic laws rather than those of the Church is not known. It is likely that it was about the time when the family left for New Spain with the governor as their patron, or shortly after their arrival in Tampico. When he was told of the change in religious status, Luis inquired whether the other members of the family knew that they were Jews. He was informed that the friar Gaspar and the three youngest, Mariana, Miguel, and Anica, did not. Luis' father taught him some rudiments of Judaism and referred him to Licenciado Manuel de Morales for additional learning.

The inquisitors described Francisco Rodríguez de Matos as a rabbi, but he did not merit the title and there is nothing to corroborate the statement that he ever had this status. He did not have his sons circumcised, nor did he teach Baltasar and Luis very much about their religion. Luis' father died about 1585. His body was washed and shaved according to the prevailing Jewish customs, and he was interred in a simple box. Luis then, at the age of about 18, assumed the role of paterfamilias.

Conditions in the colony established by the governor in the Tampico-Panuco area were very trying. Each of the settlements was surrounded, and occasionally attacked, by hostile, barbarous Chichimec Indians. The subsoil contained oil deposits, and the land was not suitable for agriculture. Winters were made difficult by *nortes* (storms) coming from the Gulf of Mexico, and summers were hot and humid. Many of the original colonizers abandoned the New Kingdom of León and went to Mexico City, Taxco, or Pachuca; silver had been discovered in the latter two places.

Isabel, the eldest daughter of the Carvajal family, was a widow of about thirty years of age in 1588. Her beauty was notable and was exceeded only by her zeal for Judaism. Her deceased husband, Gabriel de Herrera, had been a Jew and had taught her a great deal about their faith. He had died some years prior to 1580. Isabel and her brother Luis indulged in much proselytizing. They taught prayers and songs to their younger siblings and to their niece, Leonor, devoting many hours to teaching her. In 1586 or 1587 Isabel attempted to bring into a conversation with her uncle the governor, Luis de Carvajal y de la Cueva, a discussion of their "old faith." He struck her such a blow that she went flying across the room.

Shortly after the incident with Isabel, which took place after the

[28]

death of Rodríguez de Matos, the governor had his godson, nephew, and heir, Luis, accompany him on a foray against the Indians. As a result of hearing some of the details of the burial of his brother-in-law, he suspected that Luis was no longer a devout Catholic. The governor confessed his suspicions to the priest who was his spiritual director and rewrote his will, disinheriting his nephew. Parenthetically, it may be noted that Gaspar must by this time have known that his brothers followed the Jewish religion. This is evident from the Memoirs in which are quoted remarks he made when Baltasar and Luis visited him. However, Gaspar never informed against his brothers and eventually he was brought to trial by the Holy Office for failing to disclose that they were heretics. He was confined to his monastery for six months because during the trial he admitted having suspected that his brothers had abandoned the laws of Christ.

FIG. 4: Signatures of Fray Gaspar de Carvajal and Dr. Moya de Contreras

Fortuitously for the Rodríguez de Matos family, two Jewish men came to Tampico to marry two of the girls. Jorge de Almeyda espoused Leonor de Carvajal, and Antonio Díaz de Cáceres married Catalina. Antonio was a ship captain, at one time owning two vessels. He tolerated the religious rites of his wife and her family, but he had begun to be non-observant. The men took their wives, their mother-in-law and her three youngest children to Mexico City to live with them.

Luis and his brother Baltasar, left behind in Tampico, tried to earn a living in various ways. They raised merino sheep and then became mendicant peddlers. They traveled by horse as far south as Oaxaca, as far northwest as Zacatecas, as far east as Veracruz, and across the country to Acapulco, approximately a 300 square mile area. Luis learned to speak Mixtec, Zapotec, Nahuatl, and Tarascan. None of the brothers' early commercial ventures was successful. During all their travels Luis continued his studies and learned many Hebrew prayers.

[29]

Later he spent some time with Ruy Díaz Nieto and his son Diego, learned Jews who had come from Italy. Ruy, who was very pious, served as a teacher and spiritual leader, although there is no proof that he was an ordained rabbi. He confined his activities to Mexico City, while his son Diego traveled the countryside to wherever there was a group of Jews. They collected funds for distressed and poor Jews in Europe and the Holy Land (the latter custom was called *farda*).

About 1588, when Luis' uncle became embroiled with the viceroy of New Spain over boundaries of the governor's province, the viceroy learned that the governor had Jewish ancestry. In early 1589 one of the latter's captains, Felipe Núñez, was in Mexico City. Whether he was used by the viceroy to obtain further information about the governor and as an *agent provocateur* is unclear. However, he did court the winsome widow Isabel, who attempted to reconvert him, from being a convert or son of a convert, to Judaism. Isabel was a "dogmatizer." This term was used by the inquisitors to describe Jews, clandestine or otherwise, who attempted to proselytize and bring back to Judaism those who had converted to Catholicism. Felipe reported Isabel and her mother to the Inquisition; Isabel was apprehended in early April of 1589.

Shortly thereafter the viceroy had the governor arrested and then turned him over to the Inquisition. Isabel, under torture, identified the other Jews in the family. She exonerated the governor from any charge of judaizante. He did not practice Judaism and was not convicted of being a Jew or observing Jewish rites. He was, however, convicted of being a "harborer and concealer of Jews," because he had not reported his suspicions concerning Isabel and Luis to the Holy Office. His defense was that he had been away from Mexico City, engaged in subduing the Indians. He was sentenced to abjure *de vehementi* and to prison for one year and thereafter to exile from Mexico City for six years. During the year in prison he died. There never was a reconciliation between him and his sister and her children.

FIG. 5: Signatures of the Governor Luis de Carvajal (left)
and of Luis de Carvajal, el Mozo

Luis, his mother, and Leonor and Catalina were arrested on May 9, 1589, after Isabel's confessions in the torture chamber. Anica and Mariana were held in protective custody. Baltasar and Miguel escaped and eventually reached Europe.

While Luis was confined for the first time to the secret cells, the prison of the Mexican Inquisition, he had several visions which he described in his Memoirs. In one of these visions he saw God directing King Solomon to feed him honey from a vial; this was intended to have Luis become perceptive and wise. In his letters Luis speaks about a honeycomb in reference to this vision. As a result of the vision, he became known as Joseph Lumbroso (the Enlightened), and appended this name to his Memoirs and will.

In February, 1590, the father of the family, although dead, was tried, convicted, and sentenced to be burned in effigy. Those incarcerated were all reconciled and brought back into the bosom of the Church, but were sentenced to forfeiture of all their possessions and to perpetual imprisonment, a sentence they never served. However, the family did not enjoy freedom as we know it. They had to wear penitence garments until their final pardon was issued and all the conditions therein fulfilled. As reconciliados they had to cease observing Jewish dietary laws.

During the years 1590 and 1591, Luis worked in a hospital. From 1591 to 1594 he was assigned to the Colegio de Santiago de Tlatelolco, where he taught Latin to the Indians and acted as scribe for the administrator of the school.

The Memoirs, written about January, 1595, were to have been sent to Luis' brothers in Europe, who had also changed their names to Lumbroso. Although Luis stated that Miguel took the name of Jacob and Baltasar the name of David, which usage is followed here, other references sometimes reverse these names. Baltasar, known as David Lumbroso, left Spain and became a great surgeon in Italy. Miguel, known as Jacob Lumbroso, ultimately became the Chief Rabbi of Salonica,[3] which had the largest and what was considered the most learned, Jewish community in Europe during the seventeenth century. Salonica was then part of the Ottoman Empire. The Sultan had

3. See Robert Ricard, "Pour une étude de Judaisme portugais au Mexico," *Revue d'Histoire Moderne*, XIV (1939), pp. 519–520.

welcomed Jewish refugees from Spain and Portugal, and many of them had settled in Constantinople and Salonica. Using the name of Jacob Lumbroso, one of the brothers wrote at least one important book in Hebrew, *Heshek Shlomo,* published in Venice in 1617.

At the time of the completion of the Memoirs the entire Carvajal family in Mexico, including the son-in-law Antonio Díaz de Cáceres, was about to go to Acapulco and embark by ship for Peru. Details are not available, but it seems that they expected ultimately to arrive in Spain. Jorge de Almeyda, the husband of Leonor, was already in Spain, having gone there in 1590 and having become well connected with influential people at court. About 1595 he had secured a full pardon for the family but a certain sum had to be paid to make the pardon final. Not until 1607 was Jorge himself charged with being a Jew. In Mexico City on July 16, 1609 the trial was completed, and he was convicted and burned in effigy because he had never been apprehended.

During the latter part of 1594 Luis had traveled through New Spain to raise the 850 pesos (over five thousand dollars in modern United States currency) needed to pay the Inquisition for the final pardon. He stayed one night at the home of his good friend Manuel de Lucena in Pachuca while Manuel Gómez Navarro and his brother Domingo were also there. Both Manuel Gómez Navarro and Manuel de Lucena were Jews who practiced their religion. Domingo was a sincere Catholic; he and his brother were either sons of converts to the Church or were themselves converts. The two Manuels attempted to convince Domingo of fallacies in Church dogma and to bring him over to their beliefs. Although Luis was present during the discussion, he did not participate.

About December, 1594, or early in January, 1595, Domingo reported his brother and Manuel de Lucena to the Holy Office in Mexico City. He did not implicate or even mention Luis' name. Later, but prior to his second arrest, Luis was in the Inquisition halls. He wrote in his Memoirs of seeing Domingo, but little did he realize why Domingo was there.

Luis was rearrested in February, 1595, as a result of Manual de Lucena's testimony at his fourth hearing. Lucena had been unable to withstand the inquisitor's pressure, and the thought of the torture applied to make Jewish prisoners reveal the names of other practitioners of Jewish rites caused him to implicate Luis. The charge against

Luis was *judaizante relapso pertinaz*—a persistent relapser into Jewish practices.

The senior inquisitor was Alonso de Peralta. His mien and his actions were so stern and frightening that at one time Luis admitted to another inquisitor that his very flesh cringed with fear in the presence of Peralta.[4] After making lengthy statements implicating numerous other Jews of New Spain, Luis attempted suicide by jumping out of a window to the courtyard below. He did not sustain very serious injuries and later regretted his action. He told the inquisitors that taking one's life was a worse sin than lying, because one's life belongs to God. He had jumped impulsively when he saw an open window as he was being taken back to his cell from the torture chamber.

On December 8, 1596, Luis, together with eight other Jews, was burned at the stake. Among the others were Luis' mother and sisters Isabel, Leonor and Catalina. No Jewish woman had ever been executed in Mexico until this time.

After Luis' execution a report by Fray Alonso de Contreras, the padre who walked with him to the *quemadero* (stake), was appended to Luis' file. The statement was made that he had "taken the cross" (kissed the crucifix) and he said that he desired to die in the name of the Trinity. For this, according to the report, he received the garrote (death by strangulation through the use of a steel vise or cord), which spared him the agony of being burned while still alive. The garrote was also applied to his mother, three of his five sisters, and the four other Jews in the auto-da-fé. The others were Manuel de Lucena; Manuel's mother-in-law, Beatriz Enríquez de la Payba, who was termed the greatest dogmatizer of the time except for the Carvajals; Diego Enríquez; and Manuel Díaz.

Manuel Gómez Navarro, also arrested as a result of his brother Domingo's delation, had observed Jewish religious rites even while he was in the Inquisition cells. Gómez Navarro was sentenced to receive two hundred lashes and to serve as an oarsman for six years in the Spanish galleys. At the end of this term he was to be imprisoned for life in Seville. There is no report of any galley slave ever having been freed or having survived this sentence.

---

4. Joaquín García Icazbalceta, in *Bibliografía mexicana del siglo XVI*, Agustín Millares Carlo, ed. (Mexico City, 1954), p. 449, states that "Lic. Alonso de Peralta seemed to have been created by God to be an inquisitor."

Mariana, Luis' sister who had become insane, was spared until 1601 when the inquisitors considered that she had regained her sanity. She was then sent to the stake on March 25th of that year.

Luis' youngest sister, Anica, was reconciled and freed in 1601, as was Luis' niece Leonor. However, Anica was rearrested in 1643 and kept in prison while suffering from cancer of the breast, which had eaten away so much of her flesh that "one could see her entrails," according to Padre Mathias de Bocanegra, S.J., official historian of the 1649 auto-da-fé.[5] Of the total of one hundred and nine Jews in the *El Gran Auto de Fé* of April 11, 1649, Anica was one of thirteen burned at the stake.

The question of the veracity of Luis' last minute conversion is one that inevitably arises. Fray Alonso de Contreras relates that Luis had wanted to die with the title of "great zealot, grand teacher, and restorer of the forgotten law." He describes the arrival of the young Jew at the cupola opposite the quemadero and tells how he had not exhibited the slightest anxiety, repentance, or sorrow while en route. He says that Luis was hard and obstinate in his resistance to words or acts meant to induce a conversion. Luis continued in the same manner until he saw his mother and sisters, who had "taken the cross" a few minutes earlier. While his sentence was being read, they tearfully added their pleas that he convert, but "he stood there like a column of marble."[6]

The only emotion or softness that he evinced, according to the report, was his tender glance at the effigy of a Jewess which was to be burned and the heaving of a sigh. The effigy may have been that of Isabel Pérez, wife of Licenciado Manuel (Abraham) de Morales, who had taught Luis and who was the author of many prayers that Luis had learned. Morales and his wife had escaped from New Spain.

Fray Alonso de Contreras stated that not only had Luis stood like a column of marble when he heard his sentence being read to him, but that he had withstood the pleas of his mother and his sisters that he embrace the cross. However, according to Contreras, at the last moment Luis asked to see the Concordance which the friar had with him. He looked for and found a certain passage in Jeremiah which

5. P. Mathias Bocanegra, *Relación Auto general de la Feé celebrado . . . 11 de Abril de 1649* (Mexico City, 1649), unpaged.
6. "Ultimos momentos," *op. cit.,* p. 65.

seemed to confirm the belief that Jesus was the Messiah whose coming had been foretold. Luis then kissed the figure of Jesus on the crucifix which the friar had been holding.[7]

It may be inferred from this account that Luis had recalled the theological arguments put forth by two other friars on the evening preceding the execution. The two friars had advanced many biblical explanations to show Luis the error of his ways. If Contreras' opinion is to be accepted, then something that had been said previously must have come back to Luis' mind and caused him to alter his belief at the last moment.

There are, however, many aspects of the Contreras report to be noted. One significant point is that it was not filed for a considerable period after the death of Luis on December 8, 1596. The point has been made that Luis would never have used the expression "the law of Moses," as the inquisitors did, but would refer only to the law given by God to Moses on Mount Sinai. This statement is erroneous, since there were hearings before the inquisitors at which Luis did refer to the law of Moses. The existence of "a public synagogue" in Pachuca is mentioned by Contreras, but it is questionable whether the communal place of worship was so well known and "open" as the word "public" implies. Manuel de Lucena and Luis are referred to as rabbis, which they were not.[8] However, the title of "rabbi" was loosely applied by the Holy Office, which bestowed it on many learned Jews.

Fifty-three years after the execution the Jesuit Mathias de Bocanegra wrote in his *Relación*[9] that Luis was "burned alive" and that prior to his execution he had said that if there were no Inquisition in this kingdom he "would be able to count the number of Christians on these fingers" [of his hand]. These words also cast doubt on the veracity of the story of the conversion or at least show that, if there were such an act, there is doubt as to its sincerity.

Two of modern Mexico's leading historians have expressed their doubts as to a conversion. Pablo Martínez del Rio, a noted scholar and Catholic, wrote a book-length monograph[10] on Luis, the young mar-

7. *Ibid.*, p. 73.

8. *Ibid.*, pp. 64–65.

9. *Relación, op. cit.* Joaquín García Icazbalceta, in *Bibliografía mexicana,* p. 449, quotes in full: "Oh, mal haya el Tribunal del Santo Officio! que si no lo hubiera en este reino, yo contara los cristianos por estos dedos."

10. Pablo Martínez del Rio, *"Alumbrado"* (Mexico City, 1937), p. 196.

Fɪɢ. 6: An iron cross worn by penitents (found in the
Plaza de Santo Domingo)

tyr. In the final paragraphs Don Pablo concludes that there is good
reason to doubt that Luis had in fact converted in his last moments.
Alberto María Carreño[11] relates the odd circumstance that the report
of the last minute conversion was not found or filed until January,
1597. Carreño proposes that if Luis had indeed kissed the crucifix this
action "may have been a subterfuge, a stratagem to avoid being burned
alive."[12] Luis had been in great fear of physical pain since being lost in
a forest a decade earlier. And we must remember that he had heard the
heart-rending screams of his mother when she was on the *potro*
(torture bed) of the Inquisition in 1589.

Whether Luis was converted during the last moments of his life is a
moot question, and the enigma remains as to why he never made a
plea of mercy for his mother or his sisters. Luis' words, prayers, and
lessons were repeated by some of his disciples more than sixty years
after his execution. Among his disciples were his sister Anica, who was
considered a saint in the Jewish colony in her later years, and Justa
Méndez, who followed in Luis' path for many decades. Justa Méndez,
who had been one of Luis' pupils, was called Justa *la Hermosa* (the
Beautiful). It appears that an affectionate but platonic relationship had
existed between them. Justa was reconciled by the Inquisition, married

11. Alberto María Carreño, "Luis de Carvajal, el Mozo," *Memorias de la Academia
de Historia de México*, XV (1956), pp. 87–101.
12. *Ibid.*, p. 101.

in 1607, and reared children and grandchildren, all of whom were very pious Jews. Between 1635 and 1649 nine of her family were burned at the stake and others penanced for being Jews.

Luis' writings cast doubt on the assertions of some Jewish writers that within a hundred years after 1492 Jewish learning had declined or was non-existent among the Iberian crypto-Jews and that all that

Fig. 7: Victim in the Inquisition rack

[37]

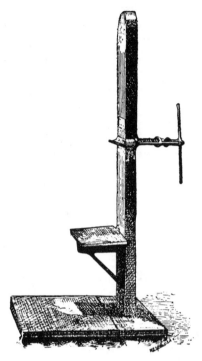

Fig. 8: Apparatus for administering the garrote
(located at Chapultepec Castle)

remained of their faith was the performance of superstitious rites. Cecil
Roth wrote that Jews were prevalent in almost every town in New
Spain and that "In many ways they seem to have been better informed
of Jewish lore and practice than their brethren in the [Iberian]
peninsula."[13]

Luis' display of knowledge, the scope of his reading, and his
thorough bilingualism (Spanish and Latin) are evidence that learning
was prevalent in New Spain, far from the European seats of Jewish
scholarship. While Luis is noteworthy, he was not rara avis. Between
1601 and 1635 there was a large Jewish immigration to New Spain

13. Cecil Roth, *A History of the Marranos* (New York and Philadelphia: 1959),
p. 275.

from Portugal, France, and Italy, and by the middle of the seventeenth century there were in Mexico many Jews who were Luis' intellectual equals.

Luis had his early education under Catholic teachers and monks. His early Christian training and environment are apparent in references to Moses, Abraham, and other Hebrew biblical figures as saints. This appellation is completely foreign to Judaism. Jews identify Abraham as the first patriarch or "our father," and Moses' only title is *rabbenu* (our teacher).

In his quotations and references to biblical sources Luis frequently used the Apocrypha and the apocalyptic books. In the eighth section of Luis' last will and testament, all the animals represent different nations that had belabored Israel at various times. This symbolism was the hallmark of all apocalyptic writers. The works of the latter were not commonly studied or used by Jews who lived where religious freedom, or at least tolerance, existed. Luis included references in his writings to Daniel, Esdras, Tobit, and Judith. Except for Daniel, these books are not part of the Jewish canon.

The young man possessed a prodigious memory. While in Mexico he committed to memory the Psalms, the Ten Commandments as they appear in Exodus and Deuteronomy, and the Thirteen Principles of Maimonides. He could quote in Latin spontaneously from the thirty-six prophets canonized by the Hebrews and from the books of Apocrypha. When he quoted from the scriptures in his testimony before the inquisitors, Luis often supplied the chapter number.

A brief summary of the Thirteen Principles composed by Moses Maimonides is here included because they embody the faith of Luis the Younger. His last will and testament seems to have been patterned along the lines enunciated by this great twelfth-century Spanish-Jewish philosopher. In the original each principle begins with the words "I firmly believe that . . ." Then follows the elaboration of the central idea:

1. There is a creator
2. God is one
3. God is incorporeal
4. God is eternal
5. God alone must be worshipped

6. The writings of the prophets are true
7. Moses was the greatest of all the prophets
8. The entire Torah (the Old Testament) was divinely given to Moses
9. The Torah is immutable
10. God knows all the acts and thoughts of man
11. God dispenses rewards and punishments
12. The Messiah has not yet arrived and is still to come
13. There will be a resurrection

There is little doubt that many of the prayers and much of the poetry Luis quoted were written by him. Many of the phrases he used were taken from or echo the Bible—especially the prophets and the Psalms. Others were the composition of Licenciado Manuel de Morales or were transmitted by him from Portuguese sources, the exact nature of which is unknown. In the proceso of Luis' second trial, and in that of Leonor de Cáceres as well as in the trials of others, references are made to a little black book and to a small, red, gilded book which contained prayers, excerpts from the scriptures, and poems. These books were among the items stolen from the Mexican National Archives, as noted in the Preface. Many of the prayers which were recited by Luis and his family and which are to be found in the proceso are in Spanish and of unknown origin, at least to this writer and to those whom he has consulted in an effort to trace their sources. Others are traditional and were well known prior to the sixteenth century. Little Leonor remembered that at the commencement of Yom Kippur she recited: "Incline Your eyes on me, O God, and listen to me because I am poor [in good deeds] and need Your help," etc.

A comparison between the Bible and the foregoing few words preserved in the proceso make plausible the suggestion that the source of the prayer is the following selection from Daniel: "Incline Thine ear, O my God, and hear; open Thine eyes, and behold our desolation: . . . it is not because of our righteousness that we plead before Thee but because of Thy great compassion."[14]

The young mystic dropped to his knees several times before the inquisitors when he recited certain prayers at their request. He did this when he repeated the Shema, the confession of faith which is recited

14. Dan. 9:18 (R.V.).

twice daily in the Jewish liturgy. The Shema, which begins "Hear, O Israel: the Lord our God, the Lord is one. And thou shalt love the Lord thy God . . ." (Deut. 6:4–5, JPS), is the first prayer taught to a Jewish child and the last utterance of the dying Jew. According to R. Travers Herford, it was the watchword for the myriad of martyrs who agonized and died for the Unity as the *ultima ratio* of their religion.

When he recited the first two verses of the Shema, Luis covered his eyes with his left hand and placed his right over his heart. The custom of closing the eyes and covering them with either hand in connection with this prayer has been traditional with Jews for over two millennia. The reason for doing this is to permit absolute, solemn concentration upon attesting to the omnipotence of the Supreme Being and to the duty of loving and serving Him and teaching His laws. The covering of the heart with the right hand is similar to a custom that had passed from practice a few centuries before 1590. It is doubtful that Luis knew of this custom as being of Jewish origin. It is probable that he placed his hand over his heart because of his youthful training.

Luis' great religious zeal was part of the tremendous emotionalism that patterned much of his life. He burst into tears many times during the Inquisition proceedings, but he never used these occasions to request mercy or leniency either for himself or for any member of his family. He looked forward to the world hereafter, as did the early Christian martyrs and mystics. He did not hold to the current, more prevalent attitude of Judaism which makes this faith a "this-world" religion.

Luis scoffed at Catholic sacraments. In order to conceal his imprecations against Jesus, he referred to him as Juan Garrido and to the Virgin Mary as Marifernández (*sic*). Due to his hatred of the Saviour he libeled him as "a swindler, impostor, and hanged (*sic—ahorcado*) man." In his answer to the indictment filed by the attorney for the inquisitors against him, he stated that he had many charges to make against the laws of Jesus Christ but that the inquisitors had ordered him to answer only the charges against him and naught else. He subscribed his answer to the charges "Joséph Lumbroso, slave of the Almighty the Saviour." Despite the hate evidenced by the young Jew in his Memoirs, nothing of this emotion was revealed in the prayers Luis recited, and there were no pleas for retribution of any kind against those whom he regarded as his mortal enemies.

The caliber of Jewish ritual of the time may be ascertained from the testimony of Luis' niece, Leonor. When she testified before the Holy Office on December 14, 1600, she was thirteen years of age. Her mother had been imprisoned in 1595 and executed in 1596, and Leonor had been in the care of two different Catholic families for four or five years. Whatever she knew of Judaism had therefore been taught to her prior to the age of nine. It is obvious that what she remembered must have

Fig. 9: Various manners of Inquisition torture
(after Picart)

been observed many times.[15] Before eating, she had to recite a prayer which began, "O Lord God, the true Creator, who never fails to provide even in the uninhabited desert . . ." She also had to recite prayers on retiring, on arising from bed, and after completion of a meal. She recalled that the Jews swept their houses very well on Friday afternoons, and then observed the Sabbath by not working, by putting clean linens on their beds, and by wearing clean shirts. On Yom Kippur, the Great Day of the Lord, which occurred once a year (she could not recall the month), they commenced to fast at five o'clock in the afternoon and did not eat until seven at dusk of the following day. During this fasting period they recited "Jewish prayers" and read from the little black book with gilded edges which her uncle had written in the school for Indians at the Church of Santiago de Tlatelolco.

During the *Pascua del Pan Cenceño*[16] (Passover), they ate bread without yeast, made from a special dough that her mother prepared. It was baked in the form of *tortas,* round thin cakes which are called matzot (matza, singular, also matzo; and matzoth, plural). Coincidentally, the Jews in modern Mexico make their matzot in the same form. They also ate radishes and lettuce at the beginning of the Passover meal, prior to which they used to recite special prayers. Leonor's mother used to slaughter the fowl. Leonor noted that all the blood had to be drained from the meat of fowl or animals. To accomplish this, the meat was soaked in warm water the day before it was to be eaten. (The traditional method is to salt the meat so that the blood drains off, but salt was hard to come by and very costly in Mexico.) While Leonor might not have been aware of the practice of salting the meat, she was following Deuteronomy literally: "Only be sure that thou eat not the blood: for the blood is the life. . . . Thou shalt not eat it; thou shalt pour it out upon the earth as water."[17] Jews were not permitted to eat pork, lard, or anything that came from the pig or any animal other than lamb. (Veal and beef were still rare commodities.)

From another source additional Passover practices are revealed. The Mexican Jews enacted literally the story of the exodus of the Jews from

15. The digest of customs has been extracted from the procesos of Leonor de Cáceres at the Huntington Library, Mexican Inquisition Documents, Vol. XI.

16. Literally, the Festival of the Thin Bread.

17. Deut. 12:23–24 (R.V.).

[43]

Egypt as recorded in the Bible. They slaughtered the lamb prior to the commencement of the holy day and smeared the blood of the lamb over their doorposts. They recited the story of the departure of the Jews from Egypt prior to eating the meal. The men wore long white garments, their belts were pulled tightly around their waists, and they each held a staff in their left hand. Whatever remained of the lamb after eating was either burned or, if there were understanding and compassionate Christian neighbors, given to them.

All the other holy days in the Hebrew calendar were also religiously observed, but there were variations in the amount of piety. There were strict adherents to the law, and there were those who were very lax. Antonio Díaz de Cáceres, Leonor's father, liked pork products, and he told his daughter that he ate them even though his wife and her family disapproved.

The Jews of Mexico during the late sixteenth century and thereafter indulged in many practices that were superstitious and that formed no part of traditional Jewish ritual. Some people observed these practices with fervor and zeal. The following are some most frequently mentioned in the procesos:

1. Beds must be made neatly, and bed coverings must be absolutely straight; otherwise the souls of the dead will lie on them and torment the owner.
2. Young girls must dry their hair well after washing and put it into a knot; otherwise no gentleman will make love to them and marry them.
3. To insure good fortune, only fowl that are either all black or all brown, without any white feathers, should be eaten.
4. A piece of matza put into a leather pouch suspended from the neck will serve as a good-luck amulet.
5. A piece of matza on top of the head can cure a headache.
6. Clothing should not be worn on the wrong side since doing so will bring misfortune.
7. Fingernails should not be cut in the normal order. The sequence has to be, first, the thumb; then the third finger, followed by the fifth; the second; and, finally, the fourth. The same order of priority applies to the clipping of toenails. The cuttings have then to be placed in a piece of paper, which is to be buried or burned.

8. One's hands should not be placed over the head. This will bring misfortune.

There have been some non-Jewish nineteenth and early twentieth-century writers on the colonial period who have included in the list of superstitions the prohibition against eating the flesh of rabbits, hares, pigs, fish without scales, and animals that do not chew the cud. They have also included the practices of draining the blood from the flesh of permitted animals prior to cooking or roasting, and of removing the suet and thigh vein (called *landrecilla* in Spanish and "porging" in English). All of these prohibitions and practices, however, are expressly commanded in the Bible.

During the colonial period in New Spain many Jews, including Luis, fasted on Mondays and Thursdays from sunrise to sunset. This custom had been in existence for centuries prior to colonial times and is still observed to this day by some pious Jews. The Jews abstained from food on these days in commemoration of the destruction of the Temple in Jerusalem and the desecration of the Torah. Fasting in general has been practiced from early biblical times as an offering to Divine Providence to beg expiation of sins, the averting of calamities, or other favors. Fasting was also sometimes observed for the souls of departed members of the family.

However, the reason for the observance of fasting by Luis and many others of this time was unique. The Mexican colonial Jews who were examined by the inquisitors during the period between 1590 and 1700 and who observed this custom unanimously stated that they fasted from sunrise to sunset on Mondays and Thursdays in expiation for their sin of deceitful living, i.e., appearing to practice Catholicism and all its ritual instead of leaving New Spain and going to lands where they could practice their own faith openly. They made these confessions after they had broken down before the inquisitors and had begun to admit their Judaism and their observance of Jewish rites.

Fasting involved no overt public act. The only persons who could detect fasting were the house servants, and they could be deceived by their masters' pleading stomach aches, headaches, or other indispositions, or by sending the servants on errands during family mealtimes or resorting to other subterfuges. We have a record of at least two men who used to take a walk in the Alameda, the public park in Mexico

City, during the course of Yom Kippur, the Day of Pardon, and who kept toothpicks in their mouths so that they could be seen and regarded as having eaten. It would appear from this that the advent of the day was known to many non-Jews.

The verses below were sung by Luis de Carvajal, the Younger, on the eve of the Jewish New Year. He and Isabel taught them to their niece, Leonor. The verses have been extracted from the original proceedings of Leonor's trial in 1600.

Much of the Jewish liturgy for the ten days from the Jewish New Year, which falls in September, to Yom Kippur (the Great Day, Day of Pardon, Day of Awe, the Great Fast, or Day of Judgment) is composed of excerpts from the Pentateuch, the Psalms, and other sacred writings. They are in several forms: narrative, prayers of supplication, and praises of the Lord. The verses given here likewise echo the scriptures. It is to be noted that the English translation does not reflect precisely the poetic rhythm and rhyme of the Spanish.

> *Let us joyfully sing*
> *praises to the Lord,*
> *for no one who has faith in Him*
> *is lacking in His favor.*

> *Let us sing of how*
> *the priceless gift was bought,*
> *while the fool without faith*[18]
> *forfeited His blessing.*

> *After Jacob had received*
> *confirmation of his birthright,*
> *he was made to leave his land*
> *with the Lord's mercy and His favor.*

18. The reference is to Esau, who sold his birthright (the spiritual blessing of his father) to Jacob for a mess of pottage. In the next stanza we read of Jacob's departure after he received the blessing; he left because he feared Esau's wrath. See Gen. 27:26–28:5.

The blissful maiden leaves[19]
with gay and happy steps,
flushed and more beautiful
than ever she was before.

With great eagerness and pleasure
she told her father that
God, in His compassion and favor,
was sending her a cousin.

Leonor de Cáceres also recited the following verses which her uncle
Luis sang on other occasions. Leonor stated that sometimes she would
dance to these verses while the entire family was assembled. The use of
"etc.," which appears in the original proceso, may have been due to the
fact that the Inquisition amanuensis was not able to write as rapidly as
the young child spoke or to the fact that he did not regard the verses as
being material to her testimony. The rhyme here in the Spanish is
unusual, with an irregular pattern.

I would rather be a sexton
in the house of the Lord
than be emperor
of this entire world.

For the gifts of this life
are poverty and vanity;
and that is why I will
govern my life, etc.

Let him suffer who has sorrows,
for time comes and follows time;
let your heart suffer,
but suffer with a reason, etc.

19. The young maiden is Rachel, whom Jacob met at the well. He rolled the stone
from the mouth of the well and watered the flock she was tending for her father,
Laban. Jacob then kissed Rachel, his cousin. See Gen. 29:1–11. In the next stanza
Rachel tells her father of these events.

Forgive me, my Lord,
for my days are nothing
if at the end of life's journey
I am still in your disfavor.

Tell me, O Lord, what is man
that You so exalt him,
that You favor him
with the attributes of Your name?[20]

Comfort him at this time,
showing him sorrow and happiness at this point,
pleasure and heaviness of heart,
all intermingled.

Until when, O God, will You not
forgive me or let me be
or let me swallow freely
or let me die, if it be Your wish, etc.

The poem of which the following is a part was recited by Luis. These liturgical verses have a rhyme scheme in the original and consist in their entirety of fifty lines:

If with much devotion each day
we should sing the Lord's praises
since He gives us happiness
and His favor in all things—
our miseries would not be so frequent
nor our adversity prolonged.
He would make us worthy of His blessings
and of dwelling in His Holy City,
where we would spend long years
free from dangers and pain.

20. This may be a reference to Exod. 34:6–7. These verses reveal God's nature in their listing of His attributes. As the Revised Version reads: "And the Lord passed before him and proclaimed, the Lord, the Lord, a God full of compassion and graciousness, slow to anger, and plenteous in mercy and truth, keeping mercy for thousands, forgiving iniquity, and transgression and sin; and that will by no means

A second example illustrates the vestiges of medieval style and is slightly reminiscent of the poetic heights attained by the sweet singer of Israel of the twelfth century, R. Judah ha-Levi. Luis is the author of this prayer, which was recited on fast days:

> *I have sinned, my Lord, but not because I have sinned*
> *Do I abandon plaint and hope for Thy mercy;*
> *I fear that my punishment will equal my guilt,*
> *But I still hope for forgiveness through Thy kindness.*

> *I suspect that, as Thou hast awaited my return,*
> *Thou hast held me in contempt for my ingratitude.*
> *My sin is made still greater*
> *Because Thou art so worthy of being loved.*

> *If it were not for Thee, what would become of me?*
> *And who, except Thee, would free me from myself?*
> *Who would free me if Thy hand did not bestow Thy grace on me?*

> *And, except for me, my God, who would not love Thee?*
> *And, except for Thee, my God, who would bear with me?*
> *And, without Thee, my God, to Thee who would take me?*

Luis composed religious verses and penitential prayers which could be used today by peoples of all faiths. The late Alberto María Carreño expressed to this author the opinion that the most fervent Christian mystic could not refuse to affirm the prayers created by this young mystic and visionary. They are heartrending *slichot* (prayers) torn from the breast of a young God-intoxicated, God-inspired, and God-fearing Jew who died, as had previous Hebrew martyrs, *al kiddush hashem*—for the sanctification of the name of God.

Luis' liturgical verses have been included in Alfonso Méndez Plancarte's *Poetas novohispanis, 1521–1621* (Mexico City, 1942) and in Jesús García Gutiérrez' *La poesía religiosa en México: Siglos XVI–XIX* (Mexico City, 1919).

Writing on fruit skins and other perishables, Luis sent many letters to other members of his family who were also incarcerated in the

---

acquit the guilty; visiting the iniquity of the fathers upon their children, and upon the children's children upon the third and upon the fourth generation."

Inquisition cells. Intercommunication between prisoners was ordinarily prohibited, but in this case the warden showed the letters to the inquisitors, who then allowed the warden to deliver them. Luis was then given pen and ink in the hope that he might thereby reveal names and data useful in ferreting out other Jews or their accomplices. Twenty of Luis' letters, which have been preserved in the files of the Inquisition, have been translated in the ensuing pages. A date or approximate date is known for only eleven of the letters. The sequence in which the letters appear is not chronological but follows the order of occurrence in the original Inquisition files.

Nineteen letters written on perishables were read into the record by Gaspar de los Reyes Plata, a warden of the secret cells. These nineteen are brief and contain no material not already to be found in the letters here presented. Some of the letters were written on eggshells. These exhibits, along with such curiosities as one of Luis' documents written with a pin on the nut of an avocado (the crevices filled in with blackening from a burned candlewick) were among the items stolen from the Mexican National Archives. There is no record of the disposition of the letters of reply written by his sisters. It seems certain that no letters came to him from his mother, since in her first trial by the Holy Office she referred to herself as an unlettered woman.

Luis sought to infuse courage into the women, to dispel their gloom, and to give them visions of the beauties of the world hereafter. He stressed material rather than spiritual aspects of an eternal reward. This may be a reflection of the concept in sixteenth-century Judaism in which the vision of heaven emphasized learning and spirituality for men, while women were to enjoy a release from earthly cares. Also to be considered is the fact that the Carvajal women had known want, poverty, deprivation, and torture during most of the last fifteen years of their lives. Throughout the letters Luis retains his unswerving allegiance to his father's faith, as evidenced by his spirit of fortitude and resoluteness.

The hopes of the inquisitors that Luis would disclose the identity of other Jews and Jewish practices in his writings were not fulfilled. As a result of the grant of the tools of writing, however, the letters and the will, penned during the twenty-two months of his incarceration, have been preserved for posterity. The Memoirs, written earlier, were found in Luis' room after his second imprisonment.

COMMENTS ON THE STYLE OF
LUIS DE CARVAJAL'S WRITING

The orthography and punctuation of the Memoirs and letters have impeded the task of translation. In the original Memoirs abbreviations were used to conserve paper; paragraphs were nonexistent, sentences were almost interminable, and many words, especially in the Latin quotations, were run together. This last defect may indicate that the Inquisition amanuenses as well as the coypist of the documents were unfamiliar with the language and were attempting to write phonetically. Luis wrote the Memoirs in the third person. The reason for this is conjectural. It could not have been done to secrete the author's identity since this was patent from the details of his life.

In the translations, paragraphs have been formed, sentences broken up, and missing punctuation supplied. The first person has been substituted for the impersonal third in which Luis wrote his Memoirs. Interpolations by this author for the purpose of clarification are in square brackets and have been used sparingly. Redundant and extraneous matter has been eliminated and its absence is noted by the use of ellipsis marks.

There are some obvious discrepancies in the documents. Luis states that he was writing his Memoirs in his twenty-fifth year, but he must have written them after November, 1594 (when he was about twenty seven) since he refers to the pardon that came from Spain in that year and to his travels through New Spain to raise money for the remission. We know from the Inquisition files and the viceroy's correspondence that in the fall of 1594 Luis was given letters to Franciscan and Augustinian monasteries in New Spain urging them, for the sake of charity, to offer him funds to help pay for his own pardon and those of other members of his family.

Luis appears to have used another Hebrew date, 5346, in two of his letters. The erroneous dates may not have been his fault but that of the copyist; the latter explanation appears to be the more likely.

[51]

There is no certainty as to the exact time when Luis de Carvajal wrote his last will and testament, but he signed it with the Hebrew date "the fifth month of the year five thousand three hundred and fifty-seven of our creation." This would correspond to approximately July or August, 1597, a date at which Luis was already dead. The Hebrew New Year fell in September, 1596. The first month of the Hebrew year falls in late March or April, but the year changes with the seventh month, which usually coincides with September. Luis may not have known this or may have forgotten it. It appears that he did not know the names of the Hebrew months.

In the opinion of the translator Luis intended to use a date corresponding to July or August, 1596, the fifth month according to the Hebrew lunar calendar. This would be a year and six months after his final incarceration began. He had been in solitary confinement and in chains for a short period. He had been incommunicado for the entire time of his imprisonment except for his audiences before the inquisitors and his meetings with Catholic theologians. He knew that his mother and at least three of his sisters were to go to the stake and that the fate of his two younger sisters, Mariana and Anica, was uncertain. He was sure of his own death sentence. The title is translated exactly as Luis wrote it: "testament of Luis de Carvajal, in which he said he wishes to die."

The mental anguish that the young Jew must have endured beclouded his thoughts. His torturous expressions and labyrinthine style resulted from his desire, under the most unfavorable conditions, to say as much as possible in a brief time. While he often failed in clarity of expression, he did reveal the most sublime faith.

the memoirs

of

LUIS DE CARVAJAL, *el Mozo*

[Joseph Lumbroso]

By the torture prolonged from age to age,
By the infamy, Israel's heritage,
By the Ghetto's plague, by the garb's disgrace,
By the badge of shame, by the felon's place,
By the branding-tool, by the bloody whip,
By the summons to Christian fellowship. . . .

—ROBERT BROWNING, *"Holy Cross Day"*

Fig. 10: Execution of Mariana de Carvajal
(after Alfonso Toro)

the memoirs

IN THE NAME OF THE ALMIGHTY LORD
OF THE HOSTS

IN MEXICO, NEW SPAIN

SAVED FROM TERRIBLE DANGERS BY THE LORD, *I, Joseph Lumbroso* of the Hebrew nation and of the pilgrims to the West Indies, . . . in appreciation of the mercies and gifts received from the hands of the Highest, address myself to all who believe in the Holy of Holies and who hope for the great mercies He grants to all sinners awakened by the Divine Spirit which He places in them, and I present this brief history as an account of my life up to my twenty-fifth year of peregrination.

First, I kneel on the ground before the universal God, sanctified by all, and promise to say in the name of the Lord of Truth all the truth and to be exact in all I write, starting [this account of] my life at the very beginning.

Let it be known that I was born in Benavente, village of Europe [*sic*], where I was raised until the age of twelve or thirteen and where I began to learn the principles of the Trinity from a relative. I then continued studying in Medina del Campo, where Divine Mercy found me fitted for the light of its knowledge one certain day which we call [the Day of] Forgiveness, a holy and solemn day among [Jews], ten days away from the seventh moon [according to the Hebrew calendar].[1]

---

1. Although not likely, this might indicate that his father had informed him of Judaism while yet in Spain and on Yom Kippur.

[55]

Since the truth of the Lord is so clear and pleasant, it is only necessary to relate that my mother, brothers, sisters, a cousin of ours from that village, and my father, all left with our household for this New Spain. [His brother Gaspar, the Dominican, had preceded them.] Originally we wanted to go to Italy,[2] where the Lord might be served best, because of freedom of religion there. . . . It must have been this moving and coming to this land that was one of the sins for which Justice [God] punished His sons, but with great mercy, as will be seen later on.

I was very ill when we landed at the port of Tampico. A very famous doctor [Manuel de Morales] also landed, who was noted for his great fear of God our Lord. He had come on the same ship, and he, God willing, attended me in Tampico until I was well.

One night, while my brother [Baltasar] and I were asleep in a little house where our family had stored certain merchandise which we brought from Castile, the Lord sent a hurricane and frightening winds to that port. The winds were so strong that they tore the trees from their roots and threw down most of the houses in that town. The house in which my brother and I were sleeping threatened to fall down as the fierce wind with terrible fury tore out some beams from the roof. The debris fell all over, causing us to hide under the bedding—a deceptive protection in our great fear. At last, perceiving the imminence of collapse, we arose. It was raining and blowing terribly. The force of the wind was such that we could not open the door. Realizing our danger, we tried, against our better judgment, to push it out, counter to the way it opened. The Lord permitted that, with the help of the wind, it be opened enough to allow us to get out. After we escaped, the house crashed to the ground. The Lord, blessed be His name, freed us on the third attempt.

We went over to the house of our parents, who were afraid that their sons might have been killed. Hearing someone knock on the door, our loving father opened it and received us with tears in his eyes, thanking and praising the Lord. Some time later, I came with my father to the city of Mexico, having left my mother, five sisters, and two brothers in Panuco, a land, or rather a disconsolate exile, full of mosquitoes, where we lived in great poverty.

2. During the trial proceedings Luis stated that his father had intended to emigrate to France, where his brother lived.

When the Lord took my father away from this life [*ca.* 1585], I returned to Panuco, where a clergyman sold me a sacred Bible for six pesos. I studied it constantly and learned much while alone in the wilderness. I came to know many of the divine mysteries. One day I read chapter 17 of Genesis, in which the Lord ordered Abraham, our saintly father, to be circumcised. [I read] especially those words which say that the soul of him who will not be circumcised will be erased from the book of the living.[3] I became so very frightened . . . that I immediately proceeded to carry out . . . the divine command. Prompted by the Almighty and His good angel, I left the corridor of the house where I had been reading, leaving behind the sacred Bible, I took some old worn scissors and went over to the ravine of the Panuco River. There, with longing and a vivid wish to be inscribed in the book of the living, something that could not happen without this holy sacrament, I sealed it [the Covenant] by cutting off almost all of the prepuce and leaving very little of it.

At this point one cannot doubt that God our Lord accepted my wish, as one can deduce from the second book of Paralipomenon, in the chapter where [Solomon], the wise king of Israel, discusses the great desire his holy father David had to build the Temple. After it was erected, [Solomon] said on the day it was dedicated, while extolling the truths of the Lord, that, although the Holy Father had forbidden him [David] to build the Temple, through a revelation from Nathan, God accepted his good intention instead of the deed.[4]

It is to be noted here, how, from the very day I received this sacred seal and sacrament on my flesh, it served as my armor against lust and as a help for my chastity. As a weak sinner on many previous occasions I now merited the fatal wound that saved me from the same sin my father committed—that of marrying the daughter of a Gentile father [his mother]. But through the sacrament of circumcision I was delivered from this sin and evil thereafter. Meanwhile I was like a sick person who craves what is harmful to him and is offered temptations to offend God. Yet, almost miraculously, the Divine Hand interceded,

3. See Gen. 17:14: " 'And the uncircumcised male who is not circumcised in the flesh of his foreskin, that soul shall be cut off from his people; he hath broken My covenant';" (JPS).

4. See I Chron. 17:3–15 for Nathan's revelation to David that he would not be permitted to build the Temple. See also II Chron. 6:7–10.

for God's mercy is infinite. Trust in God, because He is good and His mercy is everlasting.

A year after my circumcision I went, together with my uncle, a miserable blind [to Judaism] man, who was governor of that province [the New Kingdom of León] . . . to some newly discovered mines. I took along a small book in which I had transcribed the fourth book of the holy priest and prophet Esdras. Esdras' devout lessons had been one of the main reasons for my conversion. Not having the sacred Bible with me I spent my time reading Esdras in that land of savage Chichimecas.

One day of the seventh month my horse escaped with my arms, and I went out to look for it on another horse with only a harquebus, sword, and dagger that I had had at my side. The horse, although fat, tired two leagues [six miles] after we left the village. This was a very dangerous place. Previously, other soldiers had been killed by the Chichimecas who dared come so close to the settlement. When the horse tired, I could neither proceed nor go back. I left the saddle by a tree and placed the arms on my shoulder and decided to return to town on foot. However, the land being mountainous and without any road, I lost my way and night fell. I did not know where I was. I feared that some barbarian, passing by, might take my life with the first arrow. However, I placed my hope in Divine Mercy.

I had not breakfasted that morning, but hunger did not bother me as much as thirst. My thirst was so great as I walked under the hot sun before night fell, that, finding no trace of water, . . . I cut some leaves from a cactus (called *nopal* in Indian language) which has some juice. Because of the great thirst from which I suffered and the dryness of my mouth, even though I was partially refreshed my mouth and tongue remained sore for more than eight days.

Night caught me in this manner, lost and fasting, thirsty and disarmed in the land of the Chichimeca enemies and fearful of a horrible death.

However, they had already missed me at the village. My uncle had sent a soldier to the city, which was half a league away, to inquire whether some neighbor had seen me going there. The answer, of course, was that no one had seen me. They all became excited, especially my uncle, who feared that the enemy might have killed me.[5]

5. This was before Luis' uncle became suspicious of him.

They ordered that a party should go out to search for me. The party consisted of eight or ten men with a captain. They split into two groups so as to pursue separate routes. Each group had a trumpeter with it. Those who remained in the village (many of whom loved me) did everything possible to aid me in finding my way back. One man broke his legs climbing on a very high tree to hang a lamp on it. But, since the ground is so mountainous, you could only thank him for his love; the lamp did not serve any purpose, since it could not be seen from afar.

I was left with anguish and fear, as stated above, and committed myself to the Lord with all my heart and soul. As the darkness of the night and my needs increased, I heard the shouts and the sound of a trumpet echoing through the whole valley. I immediately understood that it was a signal that they were looking for me. I arose from the ground with joy, having first knelt on both knees to adore the Lord, thanking Him. I noted carefully from which direction the sound of the trumpet came and proceeded that way. I walked for a short while and this time heard the trumpet blown by the second party. I listened carefully to the sound of the first trumpet and walked toward it until I could hear the voices of the companions who were looking for me. I called out in a loud voice, and they . . . came from their horses and surrounded me, and each of them embraced me many times. They put me on a fresh horse and fired their guns. This was the signal that had been agreed upon if I were found. Thus, within a short while they had all gathered, and we went into the village.

The happiness and joy of my uncle and those who had stayed behind were great. Let us confess to the Lord of the universe, because He is good; . . . as David the Saint said, He is the one who shows the path to the strayed and mistaken. He hears those who call upon Him in their tribulation, and He shows them the way and guides them to safety. Let us trust Him, because He is good and because He performs wonders for the sons of man.[6]

I remained in that area of Panuco for over two years with my mother, my sisters, and my brothers, in exile and in mourning and sadness because of the recent death of our father. Our blind uncle [the governor] tried to marry off the poor orphans, my sisters [Leonor and Catalina], or at least bring them into contact with Gentile soldiers or

6. This passage is an echo of various Psalms, among them Ps. 137:4-5.

captains. Our father had opposed such matches during his lifetime. He did so for fear of God, because, as long as he had lived, he obeyed the holy commandment that forbids it [Jewish maidens marrying non-Jews].

During the period of mourning we were so poor that the women often walked barefoot and were poorly dressed. However, they [his sisters] served our mother dutifully and lived a virtuous and quiet life. While the family were resting one day before the mourning period had terminated, they suddenly heard trumpets and drums at our door. The cause of the din was the arrival of two [prospective] husbands that the Lord had sent for the orphans. They were very well-dressed men with golden chains hanging from their necks. God had ordered them to come and perform this good deed. They had come for the sole purpose of marrying the orphans and had traveled the seventy leagues from Mexico.

The family went to Mexico after the wedding celebrations, not only to their great joy but also to the joy of others, who were astonished at such good fortune and who congratulated the happy mother. Many of the Christian women asked her, "Lady, what good prayer did you say?" But my mother, like the good Sarah,[7] said, "Not all is due to man's merits, which are always few or none, but to Divine Mercy."

The people told the husbands that they had come to pluck these roses from among the thorns. The Lord gave husbands to my sisters, not because of their beauty, which was not much, but because of their retiring nature and purity. A few days later they all left for Mexico, praising the Lord with much joy and happiness; *orphano tueris adiutos,*[8] says the Lord; and also, *pupillum et viduam suscipi et,*[9] blessed be the Protector of orphans forever.

The news of all this reached me while I was in the territory of the [Indian] wars, in great danger of my life, since the Chichimecas were savage and dangerous enemies. There were many of them in the village where I was, and there were few soldiers with me. I thanked the Lord for this news with tears of joy in my eyes. From the moment I learned about the moving of the family I planned to go to Mexico as soon as

7. Wife of the patriarch Abraham.
8. "Orphanos tu eris adjutor" (Ps. 10:14, Vulg.); ". . . Thou hast been the helper of the fatherless." (JPS).
9. "Dominus custodit advenas pupillum, et viduam suscipiet" (Ps. 146:8, Vulg.); "The Lord preserveth the strangers; He upholdeth the fatherless and the widow; . . ." (Ps. 146:9, JPS).

possible. However, upon learning of this, the mayor and the soldiers of the village opposed my leaving, saying that they would all abandon the land if I left. The strength of God is greater than human strength. Finally, through an almost miraculous opportunity, the way was open for me to leave. This people, who were so lacking in human feelings alleged that they depended on men brought in from other places to do their labor—for this was a war-torn land. I was able to assuage them, with the help of the Lord, by giving them [a quantity of] silver with which to import more help. The day I left there it seemed to me that I was leaving a great prison, and it was really so. A few days after my departure, the Chichimecas killed the mayor but first skinned him while he was alive. I had lived previously in the house of that mayor, and, without doubt, if the Lord had not taken me out of there in time I also would have been killed. Be His name sanctified and glorified forever.

The Lord brought me safely to Mexico, where I received the blessing of my loving mother and saw my orphaned sisters. They were protected by the Lord and settled in the houses of their husbands. Instead of wearing torn skirts, they were covered with velvets, gold jewels, and fine silks. In these homes also were sheltered the other widows and orphans [of our family]. Glorified be His name forever and ever.

A year later, because of the great expense of the weddings and the many people in the household to be supported, my brothers-in-law were poor, although they never wasted [money] themselves. My elder brother and I wished, as was right, to support our mother and sisters; but being very poor and without resources, we were filled with anguish. Although we appeared to be well dressed, our needs were great. Meanwhile, our brothers-in-law moved to Taxco with their families. I was in such need that I went to serve a merchant as his clerk, to do the writing in order to have a piece of bread to eat. This poverty was soon remedied by the mercy of God.

While my elder brother and I in Mexico were still poor, we heard about a Hebrew cripple, an older man [Antonio Machado], who was also in great need and had suffered much, being confined to his bed for thirteen years. While visiting the man (as everybody should perform deeds of mercy), we learned much about God, whose divine generosity provided us there with a book the good Licenciado Morales had left to the cripple for his comfort. This doctor had kept the cripple for many days in his home, trying to cure him; and seeing that the body did not profit from the cure [he was beyond medical skill], he wrote a book for him in order to heal his soul. He [Morales] transcribed Deuteronomy into the vernacular. This is a sacred book of the law of the Supreme Being, and he also rendered into verse another thousand beauties, flowers taken from the rich garden of the Holy Scriptures. We borrowed the book and, reading it together one day, we came to the chapter which contains the curses of the Holy Law. There we saw that those truths had been fulfilled exactly. Seeing ourselves separated from the true path of the Lord, we made a pact with the law of the Lord, as a pious mother does when she sees her dead son before her.

A few days later my brother and I (we loved each other in the Lord as water and earth love one another) returned to Mexico while our mother and sisters remained in the homes of her sons-in-law in Taxco. Baltasar, my elder brother, had for a long time an ardent desire to be circumcised during the time of the solemn Pascua del Pan Cenceño. One day, moved by the Lord, we went together to the house of a barber and rented a blade from him. My elder brother took it in his hands and while we both knelt on the ground, he cut his prepuce and made a big wound. We both offered the sacrament together to God, praising Him and calling upon Him and David, His servant. Although no blood had dripped while we prayed, Baltasar felt blood gushing from the wound as soon as we finished.

We therefore left the house of an uncle [another Jew] of ours, where my brother had circumcised himself, and went to a house we rented in a lonely spot on the outskirts of the city, for we were afraid of what our poor, narrow-minded uncle might say. He came after us to bring us back to his house. Upon his seeing some bloodstained cloths, we were so frightened and filled with such anguish that we tried to explain the matter away by telling him that Baltasar had disciplined himself. A sister of the uncle, whom the Lord knew and loved, learned about the circumcision and spoke to me with pitying words. She complained because we had gone somewhere else in our need.

The house where we were sheltered was so bare that we could not find anything to staunch the blood. Not knowing what to do, I applied salt and wine, which only increased the pain and difficulties of the poor sick man without stopping the flow of blood. When I went to a neighbor's house to borrow some salt saying that it was for a wounded man, I found myself in a dilemma, for the neighbor wanted to perform a good deed for the love of God by himself putting salt on the wound. Realizing our danger, we went to the house of a man living near by [another Jew], who was fearful of God, and to him we told our predicament. As the sick man was still bleeding he [this Jew] took us [in] with loving kindness. At his house, the blood soon ceased flowing with the help of God. However, since the wound was large and had not been treated by a doctor, the patient endured terrible pains before it healed. The pains were merits in expiation of Baltasar's past sins.

After liberating us from the mosquito-infested land and the loneliness of Panuco, the Lord favored us with the knowledge of many holy and righteous prayers with which He is invoked and worshipped in the synagogues of the Israelites by the wise and chosen people of His Church. Through one of His servants [Francisco Rodríguez—no relative] who had lived in the diaspora in Italy, the Holy One brought to us in this land of our captivity the benefits received from those countries where our brethren enjoy freedom in the observance of the law of Almighty God. He [Francisco] was so poor that he had no sustenance for his household and children. And so, after fortifying his soul and copying in the Spanish and Portuguese languages all these holy prayers I have mentioned, he came alone to the New World. A brother Israelite, a merchant living in Mexico, told me once that this pilgrim was so fearful of God and detested all idolatry so much that he [the merchant] had seen him many times running into the store very fast and hiding in corners, as if a misfortune had befallen him and he were fleeing from the hand of justice. The reason for this behavior was that he had heard coming down the street the most abominable of all idolatries [a church procession and images of Christ and the saints] carried in the streets before a man on the way to his execution, and he did not want to kneel before them [the images].

When this good man returned to Italy,[10] he left his holy prayer book, from which my brother and I read.

After the Lord in His immense mercy provided for the needs of the soul, He then provided for corporal needs. In one year, without our having any money or ways of getting it, or even imagining how it would happen, the Lord gave us a fortune[11] that exceeded seven thousand pesos; blessed be He forever who provides for the hungry

10. Luis testified during his trial that the man was going to Salonica.
11. There is no clue as to the source of this windfall.

[63]

ones. Finding ourselves in this position, we[12] both decided to leave with the first fleet to sail for Italy, where we could best serve the Lord. However, we considered it regrettable to leave our other elder brother [Gaspar], a narrow-minded Dominican friar who was already a preacher and teacher in his Order.

With a strong and loving hope we went to see him in his monastery, which was near the Inquisition prison. He was a teacher of novices at that time. We intended to try to show him the truth of the Lord and of His holy law. After the three of us had sat in his cell and conversed for a while, I said in a casual manner, "I think that I heard somebody say that when Moses held the Tablets of the Law God wrote on them His holy Commandments." To this the friar answered, "Yes, it was as you heard it said." Then he took a sacred Bible which he had among his books and looked for the chapter in Exodus. He gave it to me and I said, "Blessed be the Lord; so this is the law that should be guarded." Thereupon the unfortunate friar arose and spoke a great blasphemy, saying that it was good to read it but not to observe it. He added that, even if that had been the law of God once, it was old and outdated.

For confirmation of this, he gave a frivolous analogy: that of a king who wore a cape, which he gave away to his page after it was old. Let it be noted here that all three of us were seated facing the window of the cell which opened onto an orchard and through which we could see the sky and the sun, already declining, with its brilliant rays. My other brother, younger than the friar and older than me, then asked, "This mantle of the sky and this brilliant sun that the Lord created, has it changed and has it aged?" The friar answered negatively and Baltasar continued: "So, even less will the incorruptible and holy law of God and His words be changed, and this we have heard from your own preachers. Even in the Gospel it is told that your Crucified One said, 'Do not think that I came here to annul the laws of the prophets or their holy and truthful prophecies!'" He said that it was easier for the sky or the earth to be missing than a jot or tittle of this holy law.[13]

At this the sad blind man was silent. Realizing that we had convinced

12. Luis and Baltasar. Later Baltasar decided to take Miguel, his youngest brother, with him.

13. "Think not that I am come to destroy the law, or the prophets: I am come not to destroy, but to fulfill. For verily I say unto you, Till heaven and earth pass, one jot or one tittle shall in no wise pass from the law, till all be fulfilled." (Matt. 5:17–18, R.V.).

him, he said, "Let's not speak about this any more, blessed be the Lord who took me out from among you." Both of us replied, "Glorified be our Lord and God who did not leave us in blindness and perdition like this wretched man." The friar said, "Mine is a better fortune." I concluded with *Non fecit talliter omni nationi,* etc.[14] As the poor blind one could not deny or contradict the truth that was being shown to him, he was stopped.

Then my two elder brothers listened to my suggestion that both study for a few days and that afterward we meet again, but the friar did not accept the proposal. . . . He argued that his law forbade him to inquire and to increase his knowledge. The unfortunate ones think that if they cover their eyes so as not to see the light they will not fall into the lakes of hell. No wonder the holy Isaiah[15] said of these [unfortunate ones] that they were not even capable of admitting, "All this that I believe and do is a lie." Thus their sin keeps them blind.

Since the fleet was to leave soon, we started our preparations. However, for the benefit of us all, the Infinite Mercy and Divine Wisdom decreed that, about this time, the Inquisition should take prisoner one of my sisters, a widow [Isabel], who was accused by a heretic [Felipe Núñez], one of our own nation [a Jew], to whom she had tried to teach the divine truths a year earlier. Seeing this, in fear we decided to flee and desired to take our mother and sisters with us. This was not considered safe by some friends of ours who were fearful of the Lord. So my brother and I decided to flee by ourselves, although it was hard to leave our beloved mother and sisters in danger and alone.

I am not able to describe the sad weeping of all at this parting, for it was more than my words can express. . . . When we remembered how we had left the widows and orphans, we cried and wailed bitterly during our journey. When we reached the port [Veracruz] and were about to go aboard ship, having already taken passage, [we found] these memories were so strong that we changed our minds and decided that I should go back and see what was happening and that Baltasar should wait for my news of developments. Two or three days after my

14. "Non fecit taliter omni nationi" (Ps. 147:20, Vulg.); "He hath not dealt so with any nation; . . ." (JPS).

15. Since Isaiah prophesied hundreds of years before the advent of Christianity, any such reference must have been to the heathens.

return, I went to see my mother during the night, for I dared not visit her or be with her during the day. When we were about to sit at the table for supper, the constable and his assistants from the Inquisition knocked on the door. Having opened it, they placed guards on the stairs and doors and went to take my mother prisoner. Although deeply shaken by this blow from such a cruel enemy, my mother accepted her fate with humility; and crying for her sufferings but praising the Lord for them, she was taken by these accursed ministers, torturers of our lives, to a dark prison.

My mother's two unmarried daughters who were with her [Mariana and Anica], seeing that their mother was being taken from them, let forth with such painful and sad wailings that even the worst enemies would be moved to pity. They held onto their mother, shouting, "Where are you taking her?" What the grief-stricken mother must have felt is left to the imagination of the reader. After they took her away, they arrested me, finding me behind the door where, for fear of those cruel tyrants, I had hidden myself. Those cruel beasts grabbed me with great force and took me to the cold and dark prison. I said nothing except, "O Lord, reveal the truth."

The next day, in order to let my mother know that I had been taken prisoner also, one of my unmarried sisters put some of my shirts between my mother's undergarments and sent them to her, because this was a prison where no man or letter ever came in from the outside. My mother understood immediately, to her twofold anguish. The same night that we were taken captive my elder brother had come back to Mexico and sent a young brother [Miguel] to call for me. He received the sad news that we had already been taken prisoners. . . . Seeing that half his family had been imprisoned, Baltasar was advised to escape the anger of the Inquisition. However, he remained and confined himself to a voluntary prison or room, from which he did not take one step out for a whole year until he saw what the Lord had in store for his relatives. He shut himself in with the sacred Bible and other holy books which the Lord provided him. The constant reading of these was his only exercise.

In prison I was not forsaken by the Lord. On the contrary, I received gifts and favors worthy of His merciful hand. The Lord is witness that I wished many a time to have, in that lonely and dark cell, the company of the Psalms of the prophet David, the reading of which would have comforted me; but this would have been an impossibility through any human channel. However, for the omnipotent God nothing He wishes is impossible. One day they seized and brought to jail a Franciscan friar. Let it be known that in these jails the fierce judges visit the prisoners for their spiritual comfort and to provide for their needs, every, or almost every, Saturday in the afternoon. They do this, not as an act of mercy, for they are cruel and inhuman, but because the Lord our Father deigns to give the prisoners a period of solace and rest while the cells are swept and cleaned for the visit. On one of those Saturdays they [the inquisitors] visited the friar first, asking him if there was anything he needed, to which he replied that he wanted only a breviary to comfort himself in his cell by saying the prayers of the Divine Office, as he customarily did.

They next visited me and, on finding me very frail and sad, they ordered the friar to keep me company in the same cell.[16] So it was that on the same holy Sabbath they brought him to my cell. They ordered him not to reveal that he was a friar. After we had been talking for a while during the early evening of that same Sabbath, rejoicing in our mutual companionship, the warden [of the prison] came in with the breviary and, opening the door of the cell, gave it to my companion. I felt great joy and pleasure, for I saw how the Lord had sent me, through this means, that which I desired so much—to pray and read the Psalms as I used to. I thanked the Almighty for this special token of His mercy. Let us acknowledge that the Lord is supremely good and that His mercy is eternal, for He punishes with one hand and dispenses mercy to us with a thousand. You can see from that deed what David the saint said as a result of his learning and pilgrimages: *secundum multitudinendo loxemeox consolationes tuelaetificaueuont animan mean.*[17]

Thus it happened that while I was in prison and very afflicted, the Lord found me worthy of great comforts in that agony. I was assuaged mostly through my dreams at night. One night, after spending the

16. This was Fray Francisco Ruiz de Luna, who had been imprisoned originally for having said Mass and performed other services under a forged letter of authorization. Not all clerics in New Spain were permitted to administer all the sacraments, preach, and celebrate Mass.

17. "Secundum multitudinem dolorum meorum in corde meo: consolationes tuae laetificaverunt animam mean" (Ps. 94:19, Vulg.); "When my cares are many within me, Thy comforts delight my soul." (JPS).

previous day fasting and praying, I lay down in bed heavy-hearted and despondent. I then heard a voice that told me, "Comfort and strengthen yourself; [know that] Saints Job and Jeremiah pray fervently for you." I was very comforted for a few days, after which God sent me another dream. Considering what happened afterwards, this seemed to be a divine and truthful revelation. I saw a glass vial which was covered and wrapped on the outside and filled with the sweet liquor of divine wisdom. It was soon uncovered. I heard the Lord say to the saintly Solomon, the blessed one: "Take a spoon, fill it with this liquor and give it to that young man to drink." Then the wise king did as he was told and with his own hand put into my mouth a spoonful of that sweetest nectar. The drink left me greatly comforted. . . . The veracity of this will be proved by what I shall relate later, as should be noted.

While my mother and I were in prison and in the hands of such cruel beasts, fear made us hide and deny our true beliefs and we did not confess publicly to being keepers of the sacred law of the Lord. For our difficulties and trials have reached such extremes that those who profess [the law] and confess are burned alive by these heretics with great cruelties. For this reason our fears made us deny it [our belief].

In order to investigate our denials, one Friday they called my mother to the audience chamber just as they had done so many other times. Through a small hole that my companion and I had dug in the door to our cell with the help of two lamb bones, I watched her being taken in and out. Seeing that she still denied the charges, those tyrants decided to subject her to torture. Thus they led the gentle lamb to the torture chamber, preceded by the wicked judges, the warden, and the guard. The executioner was already in the torture chamber, completely covered from head to foot with a white shroud and hood. They ordered her to undress and directed that the gentle lamb lay down her pure body on the torture rack. Then they tied her arms and legs to it. As they turned the cruel cords in the iron rings, they tightened the flesh, making her cry out with agonizing wails that everyone heard. I knelt in my cell, for this was the most bitter and anguished day of all that I had ever endured. But I did not lack the divine comfort emanating from the hand of the Lord, blessed be His name forever.

In the midst of all this affliction, He permitted me to fall asleep[18] for

18. There is a theory that Luis was subject to seizures, epileptic or other.

a while on the ground near the door. On other days I could fall asleep only for a few moments. As soon as I fell asleep, I saw the Lord sending to me a man of my own creed who was noted for the virtue of patience. He carried in his hands a big and beautiful sweet potato which he showed to me, saying, "Look—what a lovely and beautiful fruit this is." To this I replied, "Yes, indeed." He let me smell it, and, praising the Lord who creates all, he said, "Verily, it smells good." Then he divided it in two and told me, "It smells even better now." The meaning of my dream was revealed to me. [He told me:] "Before your mother was imprisoned and broken down with torture, she was good, for she was a fragrant fruit before the Lord. But now that she is torn by torments, she exudes the aroma of fortitude before the Lord." With this I awoke and was greatly consoled; the Lord be exalted and glorified, He who comforts the afflicted.

While I was in prison, I was additionally pained because I was not able to pray and fast as I used to. God gave me the chance to serve Him through my cellmate. The latter was ultimately enlightened and converted to the true God and His holy law. This was the road that God chose for the guidance of that soul and for my comfort and benefit. In the cell there was a wooden cross before which the poor friar knelt and prayed. One day, while sitting near the fire holding the cross in his hand, he placed it near the fire, saying, "My God, if I left this cross near the fire, it would burn like any wood." To these words, I replied, "Oh, you should realize in what you have placed your trust."

From that point on, we talked and discussed [matters of faith] for over eight days until the poor blind man entered into the knowledge of the divine truth, with which he was greatly rejoiced and comforted. He sang hymns and praises to the Lord, especially that which says, *mas nus Dns. ey laudabilis nimis,*[19] and he translated them into the vernacular, saying, "Great and worthy of praise is the Lord, because He enlightened this sinner." At this I danced and thanked the Creator for having granted me the special favor of leading my companion into the holy knowledge, as the Lord ordained, not only for the salvation of the poor man but also for my comfort and consolation. We observed God's law in all ways that we possibly could and with much care, and we committed ourselves to His divine magnanimity.

One day I told my companion some of the holy stories. The friar

19. "Magnus Dominus et laudabilis nimis" (Ps. 145:3, Vulg.); "Great is the Lord, and highly to be praised; . . ." (JPS).

listened to them with great devotion and zeal. He said, "Oh, how I wish it had been given to me to know the truth of God outside this prison and in the monastery. I could have learned about it in the library, where they keep all the Holy Scriptures at hand and many other good books." I asked him if they really do keep all the libraries in the monastery open. He said, "Yes, they are open, and the books are available to all for their use and study." (For the praise of God and His holy mercy, this becomes of great importance later on.) I said, "Oh, if only I could have access to one of those libraries!" The Lord fulfilled my wish with no small miracle as will be seen.

During the time of my imprisonment I was very comforted because of the light granted to my companion by the Almighty. I spent the days telling holy stories to my companion, who listened to them with great interest and devotion. The truth of the Divinity became very fixed in the mind of the good stranger as if he had been reared in it and had been taught by faithful, loving parents. Even though he was newly converted, he avoided meals with bacon and lard and all those foods prohibited by the Lord. He observed this rule so completely that many times he suffered hunger because bacon or pork sausage or some other prohibited food was served in that cruel jail. [When this happened,] he and I buried it. When we did this, we used to say, "Let us sacrifice to God," and we buried the food without tasting it, letting our hunger be an offering to the Lord with a *miserere mei* (have mercy upon me). This happened more often at midday on Fridays, because the food that these heretics eat on that day is contaminated [prohibited to Jews]. The friar acted in such a way that he deserved to be a confessor of the true God and His holy law and to wear the crown of martyrdom, as will be told.

After we were released from prison with the customary penances and garments assigned in such cases in the name of the law of God by the enemies of that law, the inquisitors wanted to separate my mother from her daughters and me, and to place each of us in a different monastery, locked in with idolaters. There our troubles would be doubled. But the Lord prevented this through His eternal clemency by having the inquisitor place part of the decision in the hands of my brother-in-law, Jorge de Almeyda. The Lord put into Jorge's mouth these words: "Sir, think before you do such a thing; consider that women are inquisitive and easily persuaded. They could easily do the nuns damage that would be difficult to repair."

[70]

The enemy [the chief inquisitor] was thus so shaken that he changed his mind and, moved by God, altered the sentence. Instead of life imprisonment, as is customary in these cases, they placed my mother and my sisters all together in a house, for the benefit of God.

I was put into a hospital apart from them and assigned to work as sexton to idols [images of Christ and the saints]. This mortified me much. They gave me such tasks as sweeping. I did this, first watering the floor with my tears; but God, my Lord, as in all other dangers, extricated me with His infinite mercy. When I had no hope left of ever again being in the company of my mother and my sisters, almighty God . . . decreed that one of my brothers-in-law [Jorge de Almeyda] should go to Taxco. Not wanting to leave my mother and sisters alone my brother-in-law begged the inquisitor the favor of letting me be their companion while he went and came back. This was God's way of taking me out of my second captivity, in which I had lived painfully, being forced to eat prohibited food.[20]

When I was restored to the company of my mother and sisters, I noticed that they bought and ate food prohibited by the Lord. They did this because of fear of their enemies and on account of bad advice from some friends.[21] I forbade this and gave them, as an example, all the saints who had consented to be torn into pieces in cruel torments rather than eat prohibited food or even pretend that they ate it. Although they had acted out of fear, their hearts being with the Lord, I did not have trouble persuading them. In tears and fear they returned to their God and laid aside all these impurities and foods. When the time came for me to go back to the hospital where I had served, an old friar came to visit my mother. He was a man of great virtue, to whom the inquisitor had committed my family for confession and to be guarded. My mother begged him to get permission for me to remain in her company and that of my sisters. This was granted on condition that I stay during the day in a school for Indians [El Colegio de Santiago], which the friar conducted. I was to teach grammar to the Indians. I was also to write letters for the friar and transcribe his sermons.

God's mercy to me was very great through this friar who loved me

20. Failure to eat would have revealed that he still observed Mosaic dietary laws and was not a true *reconciliado*.

21. They prepared their own meals and were not under the same surveillance as young Luis.

[71]

and all my family so dearly. Since the carnivorous wolves had confiscated all our property, leaving us destitute, every day the friar gave
us food from his own plate and table. Thus, through his hand as well
as through that of the enemy, God nourished us with great miracles for
over four and a half years in the den [or lake].[22] It is not surprising to
see God act that way with Daniel who was innocent and a saint, but to
see Him act so with such a miserable and sinful people [as we were]
shows God's magnanimity.

It is to be noted that, in order to grant the wish I had voiced to my
cellmate, "Oh, who would give me access to such a library," God
decreed that the friar should give me one of the keys to the library
where he kept all the books in the monastery. . . . This was a thing he
would not have done for his brother friar. . . . I had not been in the
school more than four months when the Lord ordered the friar to buy
the Gloss of Oleaster, a commentary on the sacred Bible in four large
volumes, from the library of a great preacher of his Order, who had
died. . . . He said to me, "Joseph,[23] what wonderful and rich things
we bring to our school—a gift from the Almighty."

Whenever the friar went to have dinner and the pupils went home, I
carefully took the keys of the school and locked myself in, reading and
transcribing into Spanish many things from the sacred Bible which I
stored up for my soul. . . . Whatever free time I had left was used by
the friar, who requested me to make an abstract of the doctrine in
Oleaster's *Commentaries on the Pentateuch*. . . . This was a task that
was compatible with my inclinations and liking. I so greatly desired to
do this that I would have given my life for it. Blessed and praised be
the Lord, who complies with our worthy desires.

In these books the Lord unveiled to me the thirteen articles and
principles [Maimonides' Creed] of our faith and religion, things I had
not heard of in this land of captivity. One day, as I was opening the
friar's cell with the key I had, in order to continue transcribing the holy
prophecies, I had a sudden feeling that he was coming. It was as if I

22. *Lago* means den as well as lake. Tenochtitlán was originally a series of islands
in a lake, with three principal causeways connecting it with the mainland. The translation to "den" is to be preferred; in the following sentence in the text, reference is
made to Daniel.

23. We cannot be sure that the friar addressed him by his newly adopted name
of Joseph Lumbroso, since Luis referred to himself in the third person, as Joseph, in
his writings.

[72]

were warned by God. Frightened, I locked the room again, thinking that if the friar came now it would be a signal that God advised me and was with me. I had not finished this thought when I saw the friar coming in. The Lord be praised and blessed. . . .

When my mother, my sisters, and I came out of prison [February, 1590], our elder brother [Baltasar], seeing the outcome, decided to start on his way. But the Lord first performed no small miracle before he [my brother] left the house that he had used as a hideaway. In this house that had been a voluntary prison lived an Israelite friend who had the key to the door and who used to buy the food and come in and out.

About that time a constable who knew the Israelite well came to that neighborhood, calling out . . . the name of a man who was living in sin with a woman and for whom the Inquisition was looking. The constable had heard that this man was hidden in the house next to the one where my brother was. Not finding him there, the constable thought that he might have jumped the wall into the next house. He therefore asked the Israelite friend to open the door for him, because he wanted to look for the fugitive there. The Israelite swore and swore that no one was there and tried to dissuade him from coming into the house, but he did not succeed. However, the friend found time to warn my elder brother to hide under the staircase in the house. The constable went into the house and looked all over. When they were about to leave (notice God's miracles and how He protects those whom He favors), the constable passed the staircase under which my brother was hidden; as he did so, one of his subordinates said to him, "Sir, let us look under the staircase." The constable answered, "Leave it alone; no one would hide there." And so they left, giving my brother enough time to slip out from under the stairs and hide in one of the rooms which had already been searched.

No sooner were they outside, however, than the constable changed his mind and said, "All right, let us search under the stairs." They went back to look, but the one whom the Lord protected had already escaped. The constable left satisfied, and my brother remained free by the will of the Almighty, be He forever praised.

My elder brother and the younger one [Miguel] left Mexico one night for fear of being discovered and caught by the Inquisition. With them went the Israelite companion mentioned above. They were determined to die for the Lord if they were caught. Not long after their departure I received news that they had been captured. I wept bitter tears. A great sadness befell my mother and sisters. But the Lord God had guided and protected my brothers. The truth was that they had traveled in safety for about four hundred leagues by land and then came to Puerto de Caballos (so called),[24] where by a miracle they found a ship ready to sail. The captain of this ship was also Hebrew[25] and a cousin of the companion they had taken with them. He took them from there to Spain, regaling them with attentions.

After I had spent some days in anguish and weeping, the Lord brought me the happy news that they had not been captured and that the good merchandise (my brothers and their friend) had reached the port of salvation. Confess and adore the Almighty, for He is very great, and give glory to His sanctified name, for His mercy is eternal.

One of my brothers-in-law [Antonio Díaz de Cáceres] had left for China while my mother, my sisters, and I were prisoners. The other one [Jorge de Almeyda] stayed in Mexico. After we were released [in 1590], the parish priest showered us with attentions which were no less than those we received while we were in prison.

While the mother [of Jorge de Almeyda] had lived, he was a very obedient son. God performed a great miracle not only for his benefit but much more so for the benefit of my mother and sisters. It seems that, after we left the prison, the Inquisition decided to question Jorge. Although the constable called him on behalf of the Inquisition, he escaped on his horse and did not go to the Holy Office. Irritated by this, the inquisitors gave their official in Taxco an order to arrest him.[26] One day when he was looking for Jorge, boasting very much (he made many efforts to arrest him), God sent a wild bull which they kept for the bull fights there, and the animal attacked the official so fiercely that it killed him with the thrusts of its horns.

24. Literally, "the horses' port." Presumed to be the port in Honduras now called Puerto Cortés.

25. The ship was owned by the cross-eyed Antonio or Sebastian Nieto. He was Portuguese and a cousin of Juan Rodríguez de Silva, who was burned in effigy in 1590. Juan Rodríguez de Silva and Nieto had previously brought Negro slaves to New Spain from Africa.

26. Jorge de Almeyda owned a silver mine in Taxco, and the inquisitors thought that he had fled there from Mexico City. They wanted to question him about the dowry that he might have received from his wife, so that they could confiscate it. At that time he was not suspected of being a Jew or of observing the Jewish law. Not until 1609 was he convicted of this offense in absentia.

The God of Israel moved his [Jorge's] heart and ordained that he go to Spain [about 1590] to demand my freedom and that of my family. Jorge fought with such determination in the courts for three and a half years that, with Divine help, he got and sent the decree of freedom [1594].

My other brother-in-law [Antonio Días de Cáceres], seeing that all of us—I, my mother, and my sisters—were prisoners, had left for China [prior to the release in 1590]. For the benefit of his wife and little daughter whom he had left behind, God rescued him from this place with great tribulations and no lack of miracles. Meanwhile, he suffered much and was imprisoned there. The Governor of China, moved first by God and secondly by the hatred he bore him [Luis' brother-in-law Antonio] sent him to Macao with his ship. But since, by decree of the king, the trade is in the hands of the natives and he [Antonio] had come from New Spain, they arrested him and seized all his goods. They were going to send him in captivity to India, where by no human means would it have been possible for his wife to see him again. However, the Lord, for whom nothing is difficult, ordained that he file the iron bars of his cell and escape and hide on the ship. A friend of his who was aboard hid him under the deck and brought him food until the day the ship sailed. Although he was recaptured, God took him out of this trouble and others even more dangerous than he had in Manila. These were caused by the great hate that the governor of that isle felt toward him for various reasons that I shall not discuss, for I wish to be brief and to write only about the benefits and mercies that God, the Lord of Israel, extended to me and my people. In order that my brother-in-law might return to protect his wife and daughter, God saved his life from the hands of the governor who wanted to kill him. . . . He brought him to the port of salvation [Acapulco] together with his ship, while my mother, my sisters, and I were still prisoners. His arrival was a great comfort to us, especially to his wife and daughter. . . .

I was afraid that the Inquisition might imprison my two unmarried sisters [Mariana and Anica]. Actually, they took the youngest [Anica], to the secret house of the Inquisition, but God had taught her so well, to His praise, that not even threats of torture or any other means could make her tell anything that they might use to harm anyone. From the mouth of suckling babes the Lord elicits praises to confuse His enemies.

Anica's imprisonment over a two year period, during which time she was separated from her mother and sisters, caused them all great affliction. On the days when the attendant brought her to see them and then took her back, their grief, especially that of my mother, was pitiful to see. They all begged God in a very moving way to free her and bring her to their side. God, blessed be His name, at the opportune moment heard their prayers, for great is His mercy. At the end of two years, when my eldest married sister [Catalina] and the single one [Mariana] went to have their penitence garments removed because their term was up, God granted them grace in the eyes of the inquisitors. He caused the inquisitors to release the youngest sister in the care of her elder single sister [Mariana] just at the moment when the latter was about to kneel and beg on her sister's behalf, as her mother had asked her to do. Finally the liberator sent all three of them, free and in great joy, to the house of their mother, where they all thanked the Lord, blessed be His name, for all the benefits received.

One year after my release from prison, I learned from the warden of the Inquisition that they had again apprehended the same friar who had been given to me as cell companion. The friar had broken an idol [a Christian holy statue] in the galleys to which he had been sentenced. . . . I was afraid that the friar might harm me in some way, although I hoped that the Lord would protect me. So great was the miracle performed by God for me on that occasion that it would not be fair to keep it secret. God revealed one night to my mother, in a dream, what had really happened.

When the inquisitors asked the friar who had taught him [about Judaism], he answered that it was a prisoner whom they had given him as a cell companion some years previously. . . . However, God saved me. When the inquisitors asked if he had been taught before or after his confession, he said that it was before, and thus I was saved by God from that terrible and dark prison. Praised be His name forever. Amen.

After that my companion [the friar] confessed to the God of heaven before the tyrants [the inquisitors] more bravely than had ever been seen in a man of another nation in those times. After telling them about the sayings and prowess of the Almighty and His holy law, he said, "These things in which I believe and which I confess are all the truths, and everything else is a lie and deceit of the devil." This is well understood by the king and the Inquisition dogs, but the Lord hardened them, as He had hardened Pharaoh, in order to take due vengeance on them when the day of judgment comes. Although they administered great torture and hurt him [the friar] much for this, God let him bear it all with great confidence and patience, blessed be His name forever. Amen.[27]

Three and a half years after our release, one of my sisters who hated the idols and idolatries of these unfortunate blind people, on one Sabbath of the Lord when we were celebrating a special feast, asked me to take her to visit another Israelite. Because she was going to spend that whole day with her friend, she took a small book wherein Baltasar and I had transcribed many things from the Holy Scriptures and other writings, including . . . all the Psalms and other holy prayers. She placed this treasure next to her heart in order to pray from it on that holy day. We went out at dawn, walking happily through a crowded street, when the Lord, to show how great His mercy was, permitted the book to slip inadvertently to the ground in the street. When the poor maiden noticed that she had lost the book, she was stunned and her heart almost stopped. We retraced our steps but could not find the jewel. So my sister and I returned home in great despair. Our grief was no less than that of my mother and the rest of the family, for one can imagine how grave the situation was. Our very lives were in danger. We gave up hope and considered ourselves practically prisoners and even dead people. We were so afraid of falling again into the cruel hands of the enemy that we would have taken our own lives but for the fact that we would have lost our souls.

Every man who knocked at the door seemed to us to be one of the hated ministers of the Inquisition who was coming to apprehend us. Thus we lived hour after hour, amid fear and trembling. We bought oil and other victuals, being uncertain whether we would be able to finish them. It so happened that about this time the magistrate of the city, while visiting the stores and bakeries, found in them bread that did not have the required weight [and he confiscated it]. Knowing the great need of my mother and sisters, he sent his assistant to us with two big baskets full of bread. While we were terrified, our Indian maid came up to tell us that a representative of the law was downstairs,

27. This prisoner was sent to Havana, given two hundred lashes, and condemned to the galleys for ten years.

asking for us. Our hearts nearly stopped, and fear almost paralyzed us. At first none of us went down to open the door, fearing the blow that God in His mercy might have dealt us again. Finally, still in great fear, we went down, thinking that we were going to prison. Instead, we found that the magistrate—or rather, almighty God—was sending us as an act of charity two baskets full of bread with the assistant, the town constable. Thus He filled our house with His blessing and bread that we had for over eight days.

In all our dangers and troubles God helped us like that. Always terribly fearful, I used to dream that I dug holes through which I escaped when I was about to be taken prisoner. One can see how useless are all efforts to guard a city if God and His divine mercy do not guard it.[28]

About that time I went through another terrifying experience. The Most High saw to it that some royal officials and the chief constable of the Inquisition should meet at the port of Ulua [Veracruz] to discuss matters of priorities. In order to settle their differences, the commissary of the Inquisition officiating there came to Mexico. Being a Franciscan friar, he lodged at the Franciscan convent[29] of Santiago. On learning that I had written down and transcribed some sermons for the Franciscan friars, a brother of this inquisitor asked the latter to have me transcribe a notebook belonging to a Dominican friar. This request was to be made through the old friar in whose charge and in whose school I was. It was this work that the commissary of the Inquisition was trying to arrange for me to do but without letting me know [what he desired]. He summoned me at a time when my fears were greatest. The inquisitor and his brother had planned to obtain a sample of my handwriting to see if it would please the latter for copying the notebook. Thus was I called at midday, at the request of a friar with whom I had had no association, although I was loved and respected by all in the convent. I inquired of the messenger, not without great fear and suspicion, "Who is with Fray Cristóbal?" To this the messenger replied, "He is with the commissary of the Inquisition, who is my master." I felt my heart fall in great anguish because I imagined that they had summoned me to take me to prison, but I had to go.

28. ". . . Except the Lord keep the city, The watchman waketh but in vain." (Ps. 127:1, JPS).

29. The word *conventu* in Spanish applies to both convents and monasteries. Franciscans call their houses convents, friaries, or monasteries.

I found them in the hall of the convent. The commissary then said, "Let us go up to the cell." This only helped confirm my fears. When we arrived upstairs, they ordered me to take pen and ink and write a letter in the name of the commissary. Since I knew that this officer could write well, it all looked very suspicious to me. I thought that they wanted to compare my handwriting with that of the little book that my sister and I had lost. Again I was in dire anguish and fear, as one can imagine. When I finished writing the letter, they ordered me to leave. So I went home full of an anguish which the Lord subsequently healed. He thus tested on His son the true saying ·of David the prophet that if the Lord does not guard the code, useless is the watch of him who guards it; and if the Lord does not build the city, useless is the vigil of him who wishes to build it by himself.[30]

Some time later I learned the true reason [as before stated] for their calling and ordering me to write that letter. Having seen. my handwriting, the brother of the inquisitor asked him to order me to do the transcription. They sent the book to the old friar with whom I had stayed, for me to transcribe. Seeing that I was free of the dangers I had imagined, I thanked the Lord; but I was a little afflicted, because with the work of transcribing the book I would not have as much time as before to serve the Lord nor to pray as much. . . . God found occasion to comfort me and began to grant me freedom.

Unbeknown to me, God began to give my freedom back to me in the midst of all my fears. Before I tell how the Lord gave it back to me, I shall relate a miraculous occurrence that God brought about regarding the book I was transcribing.

At that time I received a letter from my brother-in-law who was in Spain, stating that my release had been granted in writing but that a certain sum had to be paid in Madrid before the decree of freedom became final. I chose as intercessor the brother of the inquisitor. I asked him to secure permission for me to go out to collect some charity money to buy my freedom. God, the overall Governor, permitted that I be granted six months, but the transcription of the book prevented my giving all my time for that purpose.

I had arranged with the old friar who was my confessor and the rector of the college that four Indian scriveners should finish the transcription and that I should pay them. The friar had agreed to this. The Lord, in greater evidence of His mercies, permitted the old friar to

30. Part of this is an echo of Ps. 127:1.

change his mind and to harden his heart toward me, a thing that had never happened before. This friar said to me the next day in great anger and frankness: "You should not go before finishing the notebook of the inquisitor [*sic*]. It is not fair that once having promised to do it, you should leave it unfinished." . . . If I had [first] to finish the notebook myself, the six months they had granted me to raise the funds would not be sufficient. Since I was their captive, I made no answer but humbly wept over my fate. While I was in such anguish and the friar so hardened toward me, two messengers sent by the inquisitor at the request of his brother arrived to pick up the notebook and that part of the transcription which had been done. They did so because the Dominican preacher who had lent it [the notebook] to him [the inquisitor's brother] was leaving for Puebla.

When the friar saw this and considered the case carefully, he marveled and, moved by the Lord, favored me again. The provincial of the Franciscan friars knew that I had been granted a six-months leave to go out and ask for charity. Without any request from me he told the friars to inform me that if I wanted to set out on my mission he would give me a letter of introduction to all provinces, so that all the convents would help me and contribute funds. He gave me the letter after I had made the request.

Besides this, God moved the heart of the vicar general to give me fifty letters, all very favorable to me, and the governor of the archbishopric [*sic*] to grant me leave without limitation of time. Everything was ordered by His divine hand. He moved the provincial of the Augustinian friars to give me another very favorable letter, addressed to all the convents of his Order.

I tried to get a letter from the viceroy, a thing considered almost impossible. However, nothing is impossible for the almighty God who guided me. When my confessor asked the viceroy for a letter in the name of my mother, my sisters, and myself, he gave him not one but twenty-five letters with which, and with God's favor, I left my prison and Mexico.

I had spent four years of anguish and affliction in prison,[31] but I always enjoyed many benefactions of the Highest, whose divine majesty granted me favors wherever I went. It was nothing short of

31. He had not been in prison as we understand the term, but he did not have freedom or liberty of movement.

miraculous that even my enemies [Christians] were moved to give me of their possessions—money, hens, cheese, corn, and other things—with which I returned loaded to the house of my captivity, where my mother and sisters still lived. I found shelter and food in every convent where I went, but I never forgot the law and commandments of my Lord. I did not accept their food but said that I had already eaten. Many times I left the company and table of the execrated and went to eat my bread among the animals, preferring to eat among horses, cleanly, than to eat impure food at the tables of my enemies.[32]

Two months after my first departure I returned to my mother and my sisters, still with the fear in my heart that perhaps I was free but that they [the inquisitors] might be looking for me in order to apprehend me. Because of this, I did not dare to go to my mother's house until I was sure that all was well. Therefore, I first went to the house of my elder sister [Catalina] who lived with her husband and child and asked if there were any news. I learned from her that after I had left a man had come looking for me. He said that he was a servant of the chief constable of the Inquisition. This had frightened my mother and my sisters very much. I considered carefully what had to be done, whether to hide or not. The Lord gave me the courage to go to my mother's house. I found out that this was God's test, so that I might always keep in mind His mercies and might value my freedom more.

I had collected over eight hundred and fifty pesos[33] in charity from the hands of the Gentile barbarians, whom the Lord of Israel may enlighten and bring to His holy knowledge, in order that He may be praised and served by all. . . . Most of them donated all this charity of their own free will, and you could see that the Lord was with me. By that time my mother and I heard again that my brother-in-law who had escaped safely, as I have already noted, had obtained the decree of rehabilitation and freedom with the mercy of the Almighty. We received this news at a moment when it served as heavenly medicine for my mother. The joy of it brought her back from an illness which

---

32. Luis' implacable hatred of the clerics and religious of the Church blinded him to the many kindnesses they were performing for him at this time. If reminded of this, he would have retorted that they were doing these things for him as a Christian and not as a Jew or fellow human being.

33. This was not all in cash. Part of it constituted pledges.

had almost caused her death. The provisions [of the release] and our freedom came aboard the first fleet that arrived in New Spain in September, 1594, just in time, after the Lord had permitted me to raise the necessary money.

Before I tell how and when, by the mercy of God, the prison habits were taken off us, it is appropriate to mention two notable illnesses that the Lord sent my two unmarried sisters as merciful punishment for them all, since, like the sinful friars, in this life we are deserving of rewards and punishments such as bread and blows. . . .

The youngest virgin [Anica, then about thirteen years old] had a sickness of the throat, something like quinsy, which lasted more than eight months. It continued until the Lord released her from the treatments to which she was subjected. She was also crippled; and as a result of her throat having been lanced, her speech was affected. This was to such a degree that for the first few months one could hardly understand a word she said. But even then the sick one did not lack God's comfort and restoration. He opened the mind and understanding of her elder sister, the one who had married Jorge de Almeyda, so that she understood everything her sister said. Thus the doctor and surgeon and everybody else used her as a translator so as to understand the patient, whom God's infinite mercy cured, and cured she still is.

God gave my elder unmarried sister [Mariana] the dangerous illness of insanity, caused by great fits of depression. Thus her life and the lives of others were and are in grave danger. He [the Lord] who never failed us in our troubles before, does not fail us now, as I firmly believe. In her insanity she has thrown out of the window, in front of the Gentiles, all the images[34] that we kept at home, breaking them. She has said and done things that endanger all our lives, and only the Lord can protect us. . . . The insanity of the poor maiden is such that she speaks day and night without stopping. . . . In the midst of insane nonsense she also utters many truths in front of the friars who come to see her. In their attempts to cure her, two doctors ordered ten cauterizations of fire on her stomach. The pain of this so enraged her that it was only by God's mercy that she did not kill her mother and sisters with the things she threw at them. The afflictions and anguish she causes them are so great that even strangers are moved to pity and

34. The images were displayed so that Christian visitors would be deceived. When there were no such visitors, the images were turned around and faced the wall.

[82]

compassion. Many of them cry for her as if they were her next of kin or her relatives. . . .

The decree of freedom for my mother, my sisters and me had arrived with the fleet that entered the port of New Spain [Veracruz] in September, 1594. Because the Lord has always led us along the path of His chosen servants, one Thursday afternoon, the sixth day of October of the same year, and four days before the decree arrived in the city, He ordered that an Inquisition guard should come to summon them [my mother and sisters]. They considered themselves in the worst situation imaginable and wept as if they were already imprisoned and in the hands of the cruel enemy. God, the Lord, wanted them only to be interrogated by the inquisitors about something they had declared concerning Jacob Lumbroso, my younger brother, and his being familiar with and an observer of the holy law of the Almighty. The inquisitors planned to burn Miguel [Jacob Lumbroso] in effigy. After the interrogation they were sent home. They celebrated this new mercy of His with hymns and songs to the Lord. Four days later, on the tenth of October, the decree of freedom reached us in Mexico. This was the greatest of the favors and benefactions that any sinful pilgrim people ever received from the Lord. So great was our joy at this that even strangers praised the Lord with us, seeing us so happy. . . .

The Lord ordered that the penitence cloaks should not be taken off until God sent a rich neighbor who lent us the 850 pesos. I repaid him immediately 420 pesos from the money I had collected from charity. The neighbor was willing to wait eight months for the rest. And so, on Monday, October 24, our penitence cloaks were taken off through the intercession of the Almighty. God performed a great miracle for me that day. At the very moment I went [to the Inquisition hall] to doff the sanbenito, a heretic of the same lineage as ours came to accuse a brother of his [Manuel Gómez Navarro] and Manuel de Lucena for trying to lead him along the path and knowledge of the Lord. This had happened while I was staying at the house of Lucena in Pachuca, where I had gone to gather charity money. Eight days after the accusation the above-named were apprehended by the Inquisition. Even though the accuser . . . had mentioned that I was staying at the time in Lucena's house they did not seize me, because the Lord protected me, may He be blessed and praised. Amen.

The road along which the Lord guides His servants is filled with His

[83]

mercies and only with the soft blows of fears. The Lord permitted that eight days later, the following Monday, we should have one of the worst scares that we had ever had, from which the Lord freed us through His infinite mercy in two hours. I do not write of how [we were freed] or what [we were freed from] because I am still in the lands of captivity. We are on the verge of being saved, with the help and favor of the almighty and powerful God of Israel, from one of the greatest and most dangerous captivities which people of our nation have suffered. Here, by the singular goodness of our Lord, my family and I have lived in no less danger than Daniel lived in the lions' den. The Lord closed their mouths as He will close the cruel mouths which, if the Lord did not prevent it, would tear us to pieces.

For all of this I humble my heart before Him, and I glorify His holy name. I confess that He is good and the greatest and that His mercy is eternal for us and for all of Israel. *Amen.*

Fɪɢ. 11: One of the seals of the Mexican Inquisition

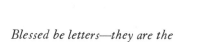

the Letters

OF

Luis de Carvajal, *el Mozo* [1595]

*Blessed be letters—they are the
monitors, they are the comforters,
and they are the only true heart-talkers.*

—Donald Grant Mitchell, *Reveries of
a Bachelor. Second Reverie.* [1850]

Fig. 12: A sanbenito with mitre
(after Picart)

the letters

———————— ◆◆◆ ————————

To Leonor and Isabel [written in the spring of 1595]:

My dearest souls, by a pure miracle pen and ink came to my hands today, enabling me to write this letter, my dearest. The first to get it may discreetly send it, wrapped in something, to my other blessed ones. I was apprehended by the will of God and His wisdom and accused by the good Lucena. In order not to implicate anyone else, I confessed the truth, and confessed it hoping for a true reward from God. . . . You, my dear souls, my angels, my blessed ones, were taken on suspicion alone, and I defended your inocence as my soul may likewise be defended from Satan and his agents by the holy angel of the Lord. I can tell you that when I alone was involved, I was happy in my prison. But once I was aware of your captivity—when they showed me my little red book and letters—I grieved and do grieve most deeply. With copious tears and heartrending sighs I plead for the salvation of [our] souls, which is what matters most.

My blessed ones, this was the will of the Almighty—and the punishment is less than the sins. Let us kneel before Him with our souls and our hearts, because He can produce good out of evil. From hard stones He can make water, oil, and honey. I understand that there are undoubtedly thirty prisoners [Jews] whom the unfortunate one [Manuel de Lucena] and others have accused. May the Lord help them all with His mercy, though our deceits [living outwardly as Christians] are not deserving of it. I am in irons, but neither these nor live coals shall take my soul away from the sweet Lord, who has unveiled before me, here, many of His mercies. I asked in my poor manner, in silent prayer before the Lord, how it is that this poor worm is worth His great mercy and how [it happens that] I can have in His kingdom a greater crown than my father. The following answer was unveiled and given to me: This will be as it was when Joseph stood before his father as Prince of Egypt and the holy Jacob took so much pleasure in seeing his son praised and honored.

I think that I told you before how, a few days before my arrest, I saw in Taxco one night [in a dream] our good father, all dressed in white, in a green field, kneeling and praying to the Lord; and when I reached the place, he came toward me with open arms and blessed me. The earth rose, with me on it, toward heaven. This means, my companions in life, that the Lord wishes my father to serve as an example for me. I do not contradict him as far as I can help. His truth is witness that I do not write this in arrogance. I know that I deserve hell for my sins, but [I write this] in order to assist those sad hearts to rejoice and be comforted—my dear ones for whom my heart is torn. I have faith that, since our good Lord has been so merciful to this poor sinner, His mercy and comfort will not be withheld from you, my blessed ones.

Remember the sacrifice of Saint Isaac: with what obedience he awaited the blow of the knife; and [remember] his faith and that of our sainted father Abraham. [Remember] how the Lord protected Joseph from imprisonment and the sainted Moses from dangers in the wanderings of Israel, as well as David and all the other saints. This is the path to the glory of paradise, where they await us. There is no better journey, not even that to Castile. And because our good Lord opens the door for us, let us not contradict Him; and [let us] have faith, even in temptation, like Tobias, and in humble patience, like Job. . . . Prostrate, I beg God our Lord that we may be companions in His holy kingdom and glory, amen, amen, amen, amen.

I was in a dark cell for three weeks. My meals were brought to me by candlelight, but my blessed God took me out of there, blessed be His name, and brought me to a prison in this yard. It has a window through which I watch the sky, day and night. What more can I say about His divine grace? That for eight days I had a honeycomb full of the sweetest nectar from the mouth of the Lord, during which time I perceived great mysteries over the heavens and [saw] the joys that await us. I ate from it, and my eyes have been opened, though not completely. Joy, joy, let the wailing and sighing cease, because great is the joy that will be bestowed upon our heads forever.

Leonor, my dear, my angel, since you are near me, send me a sign so that I may know whether you are alone. The two cloths they gave you to hem yesterday belong to me. If they are returned together, I shall understand that you have company; and if each one is returned by itself, that you are alone. . . .

There, in one of the rooms near you, is my blessed mother. Oh, how I wish that I could see you and greet you for a while. I beg God to grant me my wish of seeing you; but if not, I am comforted by the thought that we shall see each other before death, and afterward for an eternity in the land of glory, among the beautiful angels and saints. . . .

What has the Lord done to our Aniquita [Anica], and to the poor little insane woman [Mariana], and the poor widow? Oh, flock of my soul, so scattered are you! Cheer up, cheer up, says the Lord, for I shall free them from the wolves and put them in sweet pastures with their mother sheep.

In regard to Ana Lopez [another Jewess], I was with her for a few days, and she gave me news of my dearest [his family]. If I am not mistaken, you or my dear Doña Cata [Catalina] were with her daughter [Leonor], in the other yard when I sent you my pillow.

One night I was shown [in a vision] some tortillas made of wheat flour, the size of shields, causing me to understand the abundance of joy that awaits us.

Embroider on the cloths two letters, the initials of the name of the person with you. As you pass by, I recognize you from [the sound of] your clogs; and, kneeling, I beg for your help. At my window I shall always hang a cloth for you to see when you are passing by.

All sons of Adam were born to die, and blessed is he who dies to leave the long death of this life so as to live the true life. In the pen and raisins that you sent me, I saw what you intended me to see.

To Leonor [written in May, 1595]:

Sister of my heart, whom I love so and adore, I cannot tell you the comfort I received on seeing in my hands the banana that had been in yours. Believe me, my soul, if it seems to you that I was a good son and brother during our life together (but to me knowing that I served and gratified you so very little now pains me), I shall, with the help of God, be better in the greatest need. . . . My soul hopes that I shall lovingly share with my blessed mother and sisters the wheat I may have, as Joseph shared with his father and his [family]. Although you may stay in Egypt [New Spain] and I in the promised land [heaven],[1] I shall answer your petitions with deeds, my angel, as far as I can. I believe what you say, that you will love God above everything. I swear upon Him who lives forever, kneeling down with my right hand raised to Him, that I shall not do or say anything to offend Him, even if I stand at the stake; may God be benevolent and grant me His help and grace to dies thus.

This had to come sooner or later. It is not fitting for me to exchange two moments of tiresome life for eternal life, which God offers me. Notice, my sister, that mercy directed against God and the soul is cruelty. My flesh is comforted when you tell me what these men have granted you [mercy] for the Lord never forces anyone to do more than he can—neither a child nor an old man. I feel obliged to die for His holy faith and not deny it. . . . By God's mercy I am not blind. I constantly see from here your wounds and think about your sorrows; may God's hands give you patience and help. I can tell you that if the anguish of our good and beloved mother hurts you, my heart is torn by her sufferings and yours. Without the Lord's comfort I would be dead a thousand times. However, if He, in His saintly goodness, wishes to take her and us away as His slaves, I shall still thank Him dearly. So much did the Lord love Jacob that He permitted him to suffer . . . and let him hear that his Joseph had been devoured by beasts, whereas, in fact, God brought him [Joseph] to reign in Egypt, thus rewarding him for his tears.

I tell you truly, my dearest, that I am not sorry for my imprisonment but for yours. I do not weep because of my irons and loneliness but for

---

1. Luis hoped that only he would go to the stake.

your sighs, wailings, and moanings. Oh, those have torn me apart!
What help can I give you, my forsaken ones? Turn your eyes to Him
who hurt you only in order to heal you even more. . . . What can I do
to assist you, poor as I am, but to beg mercy for you, my dear souls,
from your rich and merciful Father?. . . Oh, my captive ones, if I
could only free you with all my blood! But I say to you that if I love
you so much, our Lord loves you even more. He is your Father, who
knows what He is doing. . . . I am very much comforted, knowing of
your determination, because these gentlemen [the inquisitors] are very
merciful. God sees that we are made of flesh and [knows that] even
the just man falls seven times a day. God extends His hand to the
sinner who lifts himself. . . .

You should have notified me about your companion or anything else
you know, since God was merciful enough to show me your letter. For
the love of God I beg you to tell me who is with you or anything else,
even if you have to kneel and beg that they give me a banana again.
Calm yourself, my dear, sleep and eat well. God is great, and Jonah
was in even greater trouble and in a more terrible prison, yet God
saved him. Hope was abandoned for Hezekiah's life, and the Almighty
Doctor gave him fifteen more years of life. . . .[2]

May my tears dampen the next gift of your soul. Since I have no ink,
the Lord gives them to me for my writing, blessed be His holy name.
Amen. I eat fruit with cheese and tears. I do not eat meat or broth.

———————◆———————

To Leonor [written May 26, 1595]:

My blessed one, may the Lord grant you days and hours of salvation,
amen. Oh, my mother, how I wish I could give you comfort, you in
whose womb I lay![3] My dear souls, let us pray to the Lord to comfort
her to whom we owe so much, and to cheer and cover her with His
holy blessings.

2. See Isa. 38:1–5.
3. Although Luis addressed the letter to his sister, it could have been intended for
his mother, who may have shared the cell with Leonor.

Yesterday, being short of paper and lacking time, I did not write you as much as I wished. I want you to know, my dear, that since I tasted the sweet honey from the honeycomb I told you about, I feel dew and pearls of divine mysteries softly falling on my soul. They are gifts and alms from the Sovereign's hand, granted out of His love for me. Since the Lord gave you His good manna, I repay Him and His miracles and marvels by loving Him much. Place the rich, golden crown of your love for God in your good will. Pray to Him to open your eyes and to blow upon the flame of your understanding, so that you may see and appreciate all His marvels. Notice that all that your eyes see, your ears hear, your nose smells, and your taste savors are benefits He has bestowed upon us. Make use of these for riches from God on His behalf. Oh, how your soul will be enriched! How fortunate is the creature who bestows love on Him who gave us life!

———◆———

[To Leonor:]

Dear saint, please send to my dear Anica the banana I forwarded to you yesterday, so that she may be comforted in her martyrdom. For the love of God, do not fail to do it, for the Lord commands us to divide with neighbors the good and the comfort He pours on us.

I would like to comfort you with letters every day, but I dare take only a page of paper and a bit of ink from time to time, for fear that the warden may ask it back and we shall then be deprived of this relief. It means as much to my soul to write to you as it means to you to read my letters.

The poor sister[4] Justa [Méndez] walked by my cell this morning. I would like to know whether she is in the same cell with you or maybe with our dear Anica or with one of my dear souls. Let me know of it, for I shall be comforted.

O, dear Shepherd, have mercy on Your flock. You are just to us, even though we have been ungrateful sheep. It is twelve o'clock now. Goodbye, my dear souls.

4. "Sister" is here used as an affectionate term for one close to the family.

[94]

To Isabel:

Blessed one, may mighty God be with you and with all His believing children, amen. Do not fret nor let your heart fail, for He lives and is the Almighty. He will save us from the mouths of the strong people who now subdue us, because He is stronger than they or anyone else. It was He who clothed the skies of Egypt in darkness in order to defend His believing and beloved ones from their persecutors.[5] Soon, very soon, He will redeem us by taking in His hand the sword of zeal, and His great strength will then produce marvels. Blessed be God and His holy name, for He has done much for me in this abyss.

For your comfort I shall tell you that for eight days I received a honeycomb of the sweetest honey from the Lord's mouth. I ate from it and my eyes were opened, though not completely. I saw great mysteries in the heavens, which I hope personally to reveal to you soon with the Lord's help. Victorious and happy you will be! Keep your faith strong against temptation, as did our holy father Abraham and his son [descendant] Tobias. The Lord will reveal to you His great miracles. Pray, pray, and bow and humble yourself before the Lord. Wait, wait, and He will have mercy on you and will bestow bounties upon you. For He is rich and merciful and delights in being generous and liberal to His unfortunate ones. Implore and beg [from Him] constantly. Let us be in need, and His holy majesty will then come to us. I have suffered much and still suffer for His truth which I always confess clearly and shall never deny. His truth will be our strong shield in this war against infidelity.

Blessed daughters of God, be patient and fight, for the crown of olive leaves and eternal salvation which the Lord of the armies will place upon your heads will be yours for eternity. Remember that Tobias was imprisoned while he was blind and yet his sight was ultimately restored. Regard Joseph who was imprisoned for thirteen years before he ruled.[6] Keep up your faith, for trout are not caught, etc. [sic]. I

5. Darkness was the ninth plague visited on the Egyptians because Pharaoh would not let the Jews depart. See Exod. 11:21–23.

6. Probably a reference to the fact that Joseph was sixteen or seventeen years old when he was sold into Egypt by his brothers and thirty years of age when Pharaoh made him ruler of his kingdom. He was not actually in a prison during all that time. See Gen., chaps. 37, 39–41.

[95]

dreamed for six successive nights that I walked on the waters of the sea and that only my feet were wet. There were three hunters with arrows shooting at flying ducks, but they could not bring any down because the ducks flew too high. God's voice has revealed to me that the sea is this prison, a sea of temptations; the hunters and arrows are the tricks and baits; the flying ducks are the souls of those who believe in God; and the high flight is holy prayer. Fly, fly high with it until the Almighty defends us, amen, amen, amen, amen, amen, amen, amen.

To Isabel [written May 26, 1595]:

Sequina,[7] Adonai. May joy and happiness rest upon you, dear martyrs. Blessed martyr of God, may He in His infinite mercy visit you and comfort you. Today through His miracle I obtained ink and paper to write to you. Although on account of my sins, our communications are not continuous, I always have you before my eyes. All those moments are sprinkled with bitter tears for your sorrows. On other occasions my heart is joyful, for God opens my eyes that I may see and confirm that this is the path to glory through which His goodness leads us and that around it lie the dangers of deep waters and fire, of which you have read in the holy Esdras [Ezra].

Let us not stray from Him with lack of faith or impatience. On the contrary, we must forever thank our dear Lord for the temptations He places before us poor worms. They are equal to those with which He tempted our holy fathers. I, by His grace, confess His truth, which is to me such a strong shield that not even prisons or confinement cells in which I have been, nor irons which I bear, will make me depart from it. On the contrary, His truth is more and more alive in me each hour.

You were arrested on suspicion only. You can see that it is the will of the Almighty to take you to His paradise and glory through these

---

7. I have not been able to find the meaning of this word. *Schechina* is a Hebrew word meaning the Spirit of God and His grace. If the Hebrew was intended, then it may have been part of a salutation such as, "May the grace of the Lord be upon you." The first sentence of the letter seems to confirm this hypothesis. *Adonai* is one of the Hebrew names for the Lord.

prisons, not by way of Castile, as we had hoped. Do not oppose His wishes and you will advance far along His road in spite of this steep hill. To climb it, we lean on a strong staff, that of the divine promises. Let none of you be faint [of heart]. When you feel tired and fatigued, as I have, kneel down in body and in heart and ask the Lord of fortitude for strength. He promised, in wonderful words—through His servant Isaiah—that He would grant strength to His tired and sorrowing ones. He said that just as His highness lives in His sanctuary of eternity and glory, so also He dwells among the afflicted ones to relieve their hearts and to cause the spirits of His humble people to rejoice.

He said, "I Myself shall comfort them as best I can, and I shall have mercy on My poor frightened children. Heaven is the throne of My glory, and earth is the footstool under My feet; and the eyes of My holiness will rest upon the earth and will glorify the humiliated, wounded, and grieving ones who believe in My word. Do not fret, My sons, sons of My friend Abraham, you who know Me and in whose hearts rests My holy law. The blasphemies and infamies of the oppressors will not harm you, for they will be gnawed by moths and worms as would cloaks and wool. On you will rest My eternal salvation. The skies will melt like smoke, and the earth will grow old and will tear like a worn cloth, but the salvation that I have promised you will surely be yours. It will be eternally with you—forever." Thus He said who gave us the law and gave the sky a sun and made days and nights, He who with His powerful arm parted the sea and dried a path in it through which His liberated people could pass.[8]

Rejoice, rejoice, let sobs and sighs subside, for He has promised to save us and fill us with eternal happiness and joy. He will weave beautiful crowns to place on the heads of His beloved children who believe in Him and who await and obey Him. There, there, blessed martyrs, rejoice and be comforted. I send you good news, because you, my queen, will travel, as did Sheba, from this shallow and sad earth to see the King of angels, who made the skies and the earth and who is filled with wisdom and beauty. Oh, what rich and holy palaces, what beautiful gardens you will see in that paradise where the Tree of Life grows!

You will lead lives of eternal joys. You will eat at the same holy table with your true Father, who sent you down to earth to be reared. Oh,

---

8. A reference to the passage of the Jews through the Red Sea in their escape from Pharaoh. See Exod., chap. 14.

how He will embrace you and take from His pocket of comforts His handkerchief, and with what beautiful gifts He will help dry your tears and tell you, "All is over." He will embrace you as a loving mother embraces her beloved child, whom she loves like her own life and to whom she utters a tender endearment and whom she then embraces and kisses hundreds of times, wishing she could hold the child again in her womb. Thus will God embrace you, and He will say, "Come, little angels, who, being so young, have suffered so much for Me." He will order that you be dressed in brocades or that crowns of glory be placed on your head. Oh, what feasts and dances will be celebrated on the day of your nuptials to the Lord! We shall sing there. Let us sing with joy, for the sainted David will make music on his harp, and to it we shall dance.

He blesses you, my soul. There, there, be comforted in Him, be clothed in joy and happiness, pray and repent, my dear Annas and Esthers, my beautiful Rachels, my pure Susannas, strong Jochebeds, Judiths, and Salomes [Shulamits]. Sing victory with Deborah and Mary [Miriam].[9]

My blessed my lonely ones, my afflicted ones, may the Lord's mercy send you days, good days of rest, days of salvation. Days, good days, happy days of eternal rest and salvation will the Lord send to my blessed, lonesome, afflicted ones. Days, good days, joyous days of eternal rest, days of salvation will the Lord send to my blessed souls.

To Cata [Catalina—written before May 28, 1595]:

My blessed one; may the Lord comfort you and accompany you. Whenever I cannot write you, I am distressed. The white [paper] is almost finished; but blessed be the Lord because He made pears and

9. Those named here are Jewish heroines of Old Testament times. Susanna is mentioned only in an addition to the book of Dan. (chap. 13), found in the Vulgate Bible and in the Douay Version. Salome is presumed to be Salome Alexandria, whose life and work are recorded in Josephus' *Antiquities*. She was Queen of Juda from 76 to 67 B.C. and was the sister of the great religious leader Simon ben Shetah. She and Simon were responsible for bringing the Pharisees to prominence in the Sanhedrin and to posts of influence in the kingdom.

avocados.[10] Although this takes me longer and I cannot devote as much time to my [spiritual] exercises and prayer, I still beseech the rich, merciful, and generous Lord to give liberal charity to us all. I hope that from His hand we shall receive such alms as to feed the widows and orphans throughout the year.

A poor Portuguese prisoner went by here yesterday. Her [*sic*] voice sounded like that of Manuel Díaz. May the Lord remember us all, even if we are unworthy of it. If you can, send me an olive pit, I shall know [then] that the Portuguese woman is with you; but if I receive in your name a pit from any other fruit, I shall know that the Castilian soul is with you and with us all, amen.

Look, my blessed one, very soon, when the Prince of peace comes, the holy souls of Abraham, Isaac, Jacob, and Moses will go back into their bodies, and we shall meet here. Oh, what marvelous things we shall see in Jerusalem!

———◆———

For Mother:

O, mother of my soul, the Spirit of God be with you. O, dear flock of mine, so dispersed as you are, may the Lord watch over you! O, dear mother of life, may the Lord comfort you! O, dear sisters, the Father of orphans will shelter you! Oh, mother of my heart, may the holy Lord see your affliction and guard you and assuage you. May He cover you and your children with His holy blessing. My poor ailing ones, may the Lord of the universe heal you! My poor prisoners, may God free you from prison, and sin, and jail, and hell, amen, amen, amen, amen, amen, amen, amen.[11]

10. Apparently a reference to Luis' writing on the seeds and nuts of fruits and using fruits in various ways to convey messages.

11. Notice the difference in tone. With his sister Luis was a tower of strength; but when he wrote to his mother, he let loose the inner despair which must have afflicted him from time to time.

To Ana [Anica]:

My blessed little one, my sick one, may the Lord, who holds health in His hands, visit you and heal you, amen. The Lord provides me with this opportunity to strengthen you, and thus you can see how much the Lord our Father loves you. Let me tell you, my angel, that the Lord has been very merciful to me, blessed be His name. Oh, how many joys and sweetnesses has the Lord stored up for you, fortunate one, fortunate for your illness and your imprisonment; for you will enjoy five sets of clothing of glory [worn by servants of the Lord], as did Benjamin. Strengthen yourself more than all the others, and cheer yourself up, my little one, daughter of my heart.

Thus says my Lord to you ". . . do not fear man's opprobrium, do not let prisons nor sufferings frighten you. . . . I, the Lord, shall bring you eternal salvation and shall comfort you. Rejoice and be happy, for I have taken pity on you. As your loving and merciful Father I shall dry your tears and shall turn each of them into thousands of joys. There will be no more deluges, no more prisons, no more illness; so I swear by My holy name. To you, My servants who walk among briers, on hard and rough paths, I shall give, instead, gardens and orchards to delight you. Oh, My hungry and thirsty souls, I shall satiate you with My sweetest manna and the waters of consolation that were taken from you. If I have placed you in prison, it is because you follow [the ways of] the world and do not remember Me as you should, when you are free. I place thorns on the road through which you walk to perdition, not because I want to hurt you but to force you to come back to Me . . ., to your Father, My daughters; for I live and am King of life and death. Call Me, and I shall come to you, My afflicted ones. Do not despair, for I am near you. I shall save you, My children. I give you these expiations to drive out from your souls the bad humors, your sins, disobedience, rancor, rage, and envy. All [of these] will leave you. I am the physician who heals you."

O blessed one [Anica], how I envy you all that you have and are suffering, and what a grand reward you will enjoy for your patience, my angel.

To Leonor:

Adonai, watch over us. Amen.

Rachel[12] of my life, the Almighty again sent me some ink today. It is like a miracle. Twice I have received some ink, and twice you have sent me some paper, as yesterday, when it came with the raisins. In this manner the Lord sends me the comfort for which I pray.

I heard you passing by. Be sure to turn your eyes toward my door when you go by it again. May He who reared you turn His merciful eyes towards you, amen. Since you have not written to me, I imagine that you cannot, and I have not been able to write to you either, for fear that they will discover us and take away this precious gift that God in His great goodness granted to us.

Today I sent a banana to the blessed Catalina. I do not know whether you have invited her to share your pears and avocados; but if you have, be sure that this is done with great caution, because it is so great a comfort and joy to my soul to communicate with you [and I would not want to lose this]. Blessed be His name, for He moved the warden to help us. Thank him orally, as I do.

Rejoice and be happy, my dears, for great feasts await you, as I have heretofore told you. What can I tell you about the sweet foods that will be served at your holy nuptials, what rosy sweets and relishes and desserts! If an earthly king such as Ahashuerus celebrated a banquet like the one we have read about,[13] just imagine what a feast the King of kings will celebrate. Oh, what music and festivities! After we have eaten the sweet foods and drunk from the sweetened milk of the love and wisdom of God, we shall all dance with the holy mother, and we shall sing joyously! Oh, what leaps of happiness! No sated sheep or lamb could ever leap so high!

The blessed David will play his harp for us and will regale us with his songs. We shall dance and sing with the angels. God bless you, my dear soul. Our tongues will be moved to whisper flatteries to the sweet

12. Rachel, the mother of Joseph, is considered one of the four matriarchs of the Jewish people. In Jer. 31:15 and Matt. 2:18 she is portrayed as crying in great sorrow for her persecuted, dispersed descendants.

13. The banquet of King Ahashuerus is described in Esther, chap. 1. Jews read from the Book of Esther on their holy day of Purim. While Purim is not a biblical holiday, it was most important for the crypto-Jews who compared Haman to the inquisitors and themselves to Esther who did not reveal her faith until threatened.

Lover of souls. Who can be sad when such joy awaits him? Who, having the Creator of the world to defend him, can fear men and worms of flesh? Come prison, come death, come fire! The holy fire of the love of the Lord will blow upon them and defeat them. He gave His word to the holy Isaiah, saying: "Do not fear, My sons, descendants of Jacob, My servant, My dear people, in whose hearts My law is engraved; for when the time comes for you to cross the waters, I shall be with you. The seas [prisons and temptations] will not drown you; and when you cross the fire, My hand will hold yours and the flames will not burn you." Have faith and be patient, for Zamora[14] was not taken in an hour, or is a trout caught [without getting wet—an old Spanish proverb], etc. [sic]. One has to pay a price for what one wants. Woe to him who will suffer in the world to come. Happy is he who suffers a minute here, for then he will rest all the years of eternity.

Dearest, in the beehive I saw that the sky is composed of four threads which are the four seasons of the year: summer, winter, autumn, and spring. Each thread was woven with the days and nights of each season, during which a soul in love with God must always carry His blessed law in its heart, its thoughts, and its words. Each of the four threads had five strands hanging down, three of which had three knots each. These signify the three ages, childhood, youth, and old age, through all of which just souls must walk according to God's law. The other two strands had two little knots each, meaning (first) the present century, 5346 years since Almighty God created the world;[15] and (second), the wonderful century of the Messiah, the true Christ, upon whose arrival our faithful dead will be resurrected and taken, together with the living, to the holy land to enjoy great and marvelous things. The glorious Jerusalem will then be rebuilt, as will be the marvelous Temple of God, which will measure over ten thousand leagues, as the angel taught Ezekiel.[16]

Oh, how we shall dance and sing there! Blessed be the hour when we were born; blessed be Adonai forever.

14. This seems to be a reference to the Spanish city which was repeatedly taken and lost by Christians during the tenth century. It was later occupied by Portuguese (1474–1476).

15. The erroneous date may have been the fault of the copyist. Luis may have written "5356," which would have been near the correct date.

16. The vision of Ezekiel to which this refers is recounted in Ezek., chaps. 40–45. See especially Ezek. 45:1 concerning the dimension here cited.

These are God's messages to His servants, heirs to His holy kingdom and glory. Of them it is sung, "Blessed are the just,"[17] etc. These are the trees which are to be transplanted from the earth below to glory above, where we shall see each other soon. Joy, joy, rewards, rewards, good news. Hallelujah. Amen.

Dear, send me paper if you have some. A.B. [Ana Baez, another Jewess] gives me ink. Do not send what you may need, for I shall be displeased. I have also seen the marvels of Saint Elijah's prophecies; I shall tell you about them some night when I hope to visit you.

For the love you bear me, take what I wrote to you previously and send it cautiously, wrapped in something, in your name, to our blessed sisters. O my mother, how I wish I could comfort you! God, who can, will do it for me. Look, I think that the blessed Mariana is now well. She and Catalina walked by here today, and Mariana was free and very calm. Adonai be with you all, wherever you are.

To L. [Leonor]:

My blessed one, may the Lord send you and your company days of salvation and comfort, amen. Today they took the ink pot away from me. Although I have a little ink left, it is not made with gum and does not glide easily. Therefore, I shall be unable to write as much as my soul desires. However, it is a comfort to me that I can greet you and say good morning. May the Lord grant you many good mornings, as I pray to Him that He may. Amen.

I wish you would let me know whether Leonor Días is still with you. I would be happy to learn that the two Leonors are together. If you send me a pin, I shall know that it is so. If you send me an olive pit (one of those I sent you) wrapped in something, I shall know that she is no longer with you.

Do not be frightened by prisons. Anyone who is afraid of the almighty and blessed God, who made heaven, earth, world, and sea and everything that one can see, or does not see and yet believes in

17. These are the opening words of many verses in the Old Testament.

Him, need not fear the worms made of human flesh [the inquisitors], to whom God will send death, as He promised through His messenger Isaiah. He said: "Hear, sons, My sons, sons who love Me, listen to what I tell you, My servants, in whose heart My law rests. Look up to the skies and look down at the earth, for the sky will vanish like smoke, and the earth will tear like an old cloth, but the salvation I shall grant you will be eternal. Take comfort in Me, for your goals of justice lie in My good hand. Do not fear the humiliations that men have made you suffer for believing in My law; do not fear their blasphemies, for moths will gnaw them. In vain will they dress their dead in shrouds, for worms eat through the cloth into their flesh. So it will happen to those who afflict you and curse Me. My salvation will be forever upon you. I shall comfort you, My tearful ones. I was angered because of your sins, and I sent you this punishment. But rejoice, My sons, for now I have mercy on you as your loving and merciful Father. We shall be reconciled now. There will be peace between you and Me, and I shall never again be angry at you. My anger and punishment will fall on the heads of your torturers. O My poor hungry ones, hungry for the bread of My word, I shall feed you the sweetest manna of My law! O My thirsty and afflicted ones! I shall give you seven times over the waters of comfort which they took away from you.

"Hearken, I have confined you in prisons because you follow the ways of the world and forget Me when you are free. I place these thorns on the road along which you walk, not to harm you but to make you return to Me. Repent, convert to your holy Father, My sons, for I live and am the Lord of life and death. I sent you wounds only to heal you. I purged you so as to cast out the evil that would have destroyed your souls. I made you bleed so as to rid you of faults and angers. Be quiet, for I am your physician, a physician who, like a father, supplies cure and medicine, a physician who wounds and heals. Be quiet, for I shall heal you." Amen.

Send this [letter] to our blessed Isabel.

To Leonor [written early in 1595]:

Blessed are you; may the King of the world accompany you. My soul is in pain, but so is the path to heaven. May God give you patience such as He gave to Job, to suffer with love whatever His divine majesty ordains. My afflicted one, commit yourself to God, and you will find comfort and consolation. May He lift the yoke and free you, as I beg Him by my prayers and tears, amen. If you send me a pin, I shall understand that you have a companion; and if it is stuck on a pear or whatever you have on hand, I shall know that I can express myself freely to you. . . . Beg the warden for the love of God to deliver it in your name; and if you send it, do so just as you did the salad that looked as if your hands had prepared it. May the Lord grant you eternal joy, amen.

To Leonor:

Have hope in Him and pray, for the God of Israel lives. He freed Hananiah, Mishael, and Azariah from the midst of the fire and Daniel from the den [of lions]. I cannot guess which of you sent the short letter I received. O my souls, O my flock, O my companions, may He who can, help you out! If it [the letter] is from Anica, you are not guilty, my dear, nor is any one of you guilty, for you have done penance for the past. Apparently the Lord's will is to take us to heaven and not to Castile. I consider this a worthier journey, better than dying a thousand deaths every day and offending the true God, who gave counsel to Susanna. May He give you counsel and salvation, amen, amen, amen, amen, amen, amen. Sister of my heart, may Almighty God give you counsel and free your soul and life, for He is God and He can! Amen.

I only confessed of God's truth concerning myself, hoping for the prize of paradise and eternal glory. You, my dearest, were arrested on suspicion only. I have not given false testimony against anyone, thank God. What can I tell you? You are not guilty; but anyway I think it is useless to make denial. If you plead for mercy, I think they will grant it to you for the second time, if you do not dare to leap to heaven through the path of death. Death must come sooner or later, be it in your own bed or house or as a consequence of the trial.

That is why I have chosen, with the help of the blessed God—may He be favorable to me—to die for His holy law—so as to live eternally. I pray that the Lord of fortitude will advise you best, amen. If the poor lunatic in her madness has not told lies about you, they have no witnesses to harm you.

——————◆——————

To Catalina [apparently written in the early summer of 1595]:

God's blessed, gift of my life, may the sweet God visit you and comfort you. Through a miracle of His, and not the first one He has performed for this sinner here, I received some ink so that I can write to you. I was arrested by the will of the Highest and accused by the good Lucena. Although I pretended otherwise in front of you all, the truth is that my heart never parted from the law of God. So I have confessed and do confess concerning myself alone, because to say otherwise would be to give false testimony.

You were arrested, my angels, on suspicion only. But I have defended and do defend your innocence, as a true brother. When I alone was in jail, my imprisonment was like a lark to me. Now that I know that you also are imprisoned, my soul is very afflicted. If only I knew that you bear it [your confinement] for love of God and with patience, I would exult joyously. Blessed is he who suffers while drawing the breath of mortal life, for he will enjoy eternal peace in heaven. There is no way to heaven other than through worries and sufferings. He who does not suffer here will have to forget about the glory [of the hereafter].

My angel, remember this and act accordingly. For all the saints who await us in heaven suffered while they were mortals; and if our sweet Father wishes to do so much good for us, let us not be impatient. Abraham tied his son's feet and hands; and the blessed Isaac, in marvelous obedience, awaited the slash of the knife. Have hope, for the angel of God entered and stayed Abraham's hand and brought a ram as an offering to God in place of Isaac. He did not want Isaac's life, but [He wanted to test] Abraham's fortitude against temptations. So He does with you. He does not desire a long or tortuous road to death but rather [to give] the gift of eternal life. Have faith like that of Sarah, who in her old age bore a son. God has power to transform your tears into laughter. Kneel before Him in penance with Asenec,[18] for He will not deny you His comfort. Pray, pray, as Anna and Esther did in danger; hope as did the blessed Judith and Salome.

Dear martyr, nail the tempting enemies' temples, as did Jael to Sisera.[19] You will come out of this Egypt of our prisons. You will sing victoriously with Mary and Deborah in paradise, where they await you to dance [with them] and where the Lord will crown you. There, my wailing ones, take comfort. You are going, as Queen Sheba did, to visit the beautiful and wise King of angels, to see His rich palaces and gardens and paradise, and to eat His sweet foods. Oh, what beautiful skirts and jackets and capes and garlands from the finest gold of glory He will give you! You will be bathed in perfumed waters. How joyously we shall dance and sing with Him, what feasting, what dances, what leaps of joy! How the blessed Father, whom you awaited and believed in, will embrace you!

If you will lift up your eyes to see those joys, everything else here will seem refuse and smoke. May the good Lord open your eyes as He opened the eyes of the saintly Tobias, and [may He] heal and free you as He did Sarah.

Joseph was in prison for thirteen years, only to rule afterwards. The God who freed Daniel from the den and the three saints [Hananiah, Mishael, and Azariah] from the fire is living. He has given us His word that He will save us if we have faith and patience such as the Lord gave to Job. May He grant it to you and to us, too, amen. If only I could tell you what the blessed God has done for me! They held me for

18. Possibly a reference to Asenath, daughter of Potiphera, priest of On. The then-ruling Pharaoh gave her to Joseph for his wife when he made Joseph his Grand Vizier. See Gen. 41:45. A Greek Apocrypha of decidedly Jewish character, the *Life and Confession or Prayer of Asenath,* relates that Asenath, after falling in love with Joseph, repented of her worship of idols and spent eight days fasting and doing penance. She later became the mother of Ephraim and Manasseh. Every Friday evening when they say the prayers inaugurating the Sabbath, Jewish orthodox fathers bless their sons, praying that they may be like Manasseh and Ephraim.

19. Jael was the wife of Heber the Kenite. She slew Sisera, leader of the armies of Jabin, by driving a tentpin through his temples while he slept. See Judges, chap. 4.

three weeks in a dark cell and brought down my meals by candlelight. His holy hand has taken me out of that place, and now I am able to see the sky day and night through a little window, where I shall hang a piece of cloth for you to see, blessed one, when you are passing by.

For eight days I had a beehive full of honey from the sweet mouth of the Almighty. I ate from it and have seen and experienced great mysteries. Oh, how I wish I could tell you about them. I hope that the Lord will let me see you some night soon, in order to comfort you personally. I am now in irons, which are taken off me once a week to enable me to wash. But no irons can separate me from the good, sweet Father, for He has chained my soul with the golden and bejeweled chain of His love. Be patient, for our Lord will come soon. He has promised me in His good words that our glory will soon come. There, there, above this steep hill of our prison we shall find our glory.

Our Lord awaits us there. Oh, what tournaments and parties will be celebrated in the true kingdom upon our arrival! Blessed be the day you were born, the bread you have eaten, and the water you have drunk, for you will see our Lord and King! Do not go to Him empty-handed, but take along the fragrant bouquet of lively flowers of faith, patience, and prayer from these prisons. I pray that the Lord will grant us grace, amen.

———◆———

To Leonor:

My soul, if you have white paper on which to write me a short note, but no ink, light a candle and place a plate over the flame, and then use a straw with the soot that has accumulated, to write with instead of ink. Inform me whether you are alone and whether you know anything about our blessed lamb, our mother. Is she there, too? I sent her the raisins you had sent to me, but the warden took them upstairs. If you only knew how painful to my flesh was the [sight of the] penholder [the proof he received that they were also in prison], but what great comfort it has given to my soul! Since we have all been companions in our anguish and sorrows, we shall also be companions in death and unto glory. Until I saw the pen I thought I would leave [die] alone, but now I know that your souls will be with me. The Lord grants us all His generous mercy, for which we should thank Him; have patience, blessed be His name.

We have to wait only a little longer. There, there, be strong. Have hope like that of Judith and Salome; trust as Susanna did when she was taken to her unfair death[20]; do penance, as Asenec [Asenath] did; and pray humbly, as Esther did. Have faith like that of your mother Sarah, who bore a child in her old age. The Lord reaps victory out of danger and strife. You must nail down Satan and his temptations, as Jael nailed Sisera, and you will sing to the Almighty all the beautiful songs. You, dearest souls, will escape from Egypt, the deluge, and the seas with Mary and Deborah, who await you in heaven. They will take you, amid dances and songs, to receive the crown of eternal glory and the blessings of the Lord. Oh, how little we suffer here compared to the reward that awaits us when a new gentleman or a new religious soul enters that rich city where the King of angels and emperors reigns, to proclaim the holy religion of the most blessed Lord. The angels and saints will organize gorgeous tournaments and great jousts and feasts.

There, there, my queens, crowned by Him, blessed be the day you were born, the bread you ate, the earth you stepped on, the torture you have endured, and the womb from which you were born. You will go, as did Sheba the Queen from her lowlands, to visit the holy court and city of Jerusalem, to see the King of kings and Lord of lords, to visit the rich palaces, its orchards, its gardens, its paradise; to taste of its wisdom and beauty, to see His lovely attendants, who are the innumerable angels and saints.

Bring offerings to place at His feet when you kneel before Him; bring Him your forbearance in prison, [a virtue] which smells better than myrrh and makes the soul immortal; bring Him a fragrant bouquet of your piety; but take care that it is beautiful, and see to it that it has in it flowers of all colors and carnations of faith, hope, charity, patience, humility, meekness, innocence, chastity and perseverance. These are the flowers of paradise that never wilt, whose fragrance, even amid thorns and thistles, reaches the Almighty. Oh, how thankful He

20. The story of Susanna and the elders who unjustly accused her of immorality and the account of her subsequent vindication and release from a death sentence are given in an addition to the Book of Daniel found in the Vulgate Bible and the Douay Version. See Dan., chap. 13, D.V.

will be for your present, and how He will bless you, saying, "Eternal glory and life be unto you, My daughters." How envious of you would I be were I to stay behind.

My children, the Lord does not forget your penance, your prayers, and fasts. He has brought you here to grant you a reward for it all. He remembers well how you went barefoot on the cold earth, receiving charity in hospitals. He has told me that He will thank you just as a loving father and mother do who hear their baby say something funny and witty, and embrace and kiss him thousands of times. There, my weeping ones, you have a good Father who will wipe away your tears with the handkerchief of comfort and embrace you and love you. My good Shepherd of Israel, for whose love my soul burns, will tell you, "There, My sheep, show me where the dog bit you"; and you will answer Him joyously, "My Lord and Father, his bite reached our very soul—be it to his damnation. He came across our path and bit us a thousand times." Because we invoked His name and obeyed His orders and His laws, [the good God will say:] "My daughters, I shall heal and avenge you with a thousand kisses and embraces. Here, put on this rich chain, which will bind you forever to My love. Angels, fetch the beautiful gowns I have ordered for My daughters and spouses. Give them skirts of white satin in exchange for their cotton ones; dress them in brocade jackets, and attire them well with rich headdresses and garlands. Let no finger be without a ring, for they suffered much for Me. But before all this, bathe them in perfumed waters, for they shall sit and eat at My table." Amen. Oh, what a beautiful future there is in store for you. I have no ink left. Hallelujah.

To Leonor [written before June 1, 1595]:

Sequina rest upon us, amen. May the Lord grant days of grace, comfort, and salvation to you and your unfortunate and afflicted company, amen. The great love I have for you does not let a day pass without my writing to you. Blessed be Adonai forever, for He grants us miraculously this consolation in our abyss. I did not send more than a good morning greeting on the banana yesterday, and that is why I did not address it specifically to you. It seems to me natural that, because yours is the largest share of my great love, you should be jealous; for jealousy is the smoke from the flames of love. May the love of God burn forever in our souls. Amen.

My dear pilgrim headed for glory, where all the good in the world is, I have seen fit to send you a staff [a prayer] on which you may lean on your way up, in the name of the Lord. This staff was taken from the paradise of the Holy Scriptures. Engrave it in your memory, say it daily, and with the Lord's help you will not fall into temptations. The Lord tested Abraham and told him, "Abraham, Abraham, take your beloved son Isaac and sacrifice him to Me on one of the mountains which I shall indicate to you." At His command our holy father Abraham awoke early, before sunrise, made his ass ready, cut up wood for the sacrifice, and took with him his son Isaac and two of his house servants. They climbed Mount Moriah, where many years later the holy Temple of the Lord was to be erected.

Abraham told his servants to wait at the foot of the mountain while he and his son went up to adore the Lord. Then, [Abraham] having placed the wood on his beloved son's back and having taken the fire in one hand and the knife in the other, they both climbed up (may the Lord permit us to climb, following in their holy footsteps). Isaac asked his father, "Father, why is it that we are carrying a knife and wood and fire but not the animal we shall offer to the Lord?" To this Abraham replied, "The Lord will supply us with the proper victim, my son." (May the Lord, as He provided then, provide us with faith, patience, and obedience because of [our] love of Him.)

Once they were at the summit of the mountain, Abraham tied his son's feet and hands. Placing him upon the wood on the altar, he was about to draw the knife when suddenly the Angel of the Lord stayed his hand, saying: "Abraham, Abraham, do not touch your son. It is not

My will that Isaac should die, but [My will is] to reward you with eternal worthiness in My eyes; you have shown Me how much you love and fear Me, for you did not spare even your son's life for love of Me."[21] Then Abraham saw the ram which the Lord supplied and offered the animal instead of his son. After the sacrifice the Angel of the Lord again spoke to Abraham and said: "I swear in My own name that the Lord says: 'What you have done and were ready to do for Me will not remain without reward, for I shall give you as many children as there are grains of sand on the seashore and as many as the stars that shine in the sky. Your descendants will enter the gates of their enemies (that is, through the king Messiah). Blessed will be all your generations on earth.' "[22] Abraham believed in the Lord's word and worshipped Him; He [the Angel] then said to Isaac: "You have obeyed My command and were willing to die, and for this reason all the Lord's blessings will be fulfilled in you, blessed be Adonai."

I have many more mysteries to speak to you about, but it is twelve o'clock, and I would need many pages of paper. Even many pages would not be enough; so I am only writing for the present what I can.

Remember that the Lord leads His beloved ones through temptations and permits them to attain victories after wars. Tobias was blinded after he had done so much good and then was healed by the Lord. The Angel told him: "Even though you were loved and were pleasing to the Lord, He found you fit to be tested with temptations." My dears, when the burden of prison and anguish bears down on you, kneel down before the Lord and beseech Him to lessen your burden in consideration of the burden that Isaac carried up the mountain.

Pray that He may help you to carry your burden and grant you faith and steadfastness, so that He does not let you fall even once. Pray not

21. See Gen. 22:11–12, where the text reads: "And the Angel of the Lord called unto him out of heaven and said: 'Abraham, Abraham.' And he said: 'Here am I.' And he said: 'Lay not thy hand upon the lad, neither do thou any thing unto him; for now I know that thou art a God-fearing man, seeing thou hast not withheld thy son, thine only son, from Me.' " (JPS).

22. This portion is close to the text of Gen. 22:16–18, which reads: ". . . 'By Myself have I sworn, saieth the Lord, because thou hast done this thing, and hast not withheld thy son, thine only son, that in blessing I will bless thee, and in multiplying I will multiply thy seed as the stars of the heaven, and as the sand which is upon the seashore; and thy seed shall possess the gate of his enemies; and in thy seed shall all the nations of the earth be blessed; because thou hast hearkened to My voice'." (JPS).

only for yourself but for all around you, for the Lord is generous, and He commanded us to help the fallen. Beg Him to extend His hand to you, and He will do so. Remember Abraham's faith and devotion. Someone else in his case would have said to God, "Well, is this why You gave me a son in my old age?" But Abraham did not open his mouth, and while he was tying his son's hands, the Angel of the Lord tied the ram that the Lord supplied for the sacrifice.

And remember what a wonderful reward Abraham received: as many children as there are stars and grains of sand. Oh, my beloved, how little is our suffering, and what a great reward we shall receive from the Lord. I swear to you that only the other night I saw you in my dreams, dressed in beautiful garments with gold trimmings, and with a long beautiful necklace on your neck. I pray to see your blessed souls dressed up like that, all in glory, if you have faith, amen, amen.

To Anica [dated June 4, probably 1595, possibly 1596]:

Ana, dear, my blessed one, apple of my eye, and soul of my heart. May the strong God and Lord visit you and strengthen you and all the rest, just as this sinner begs Him, day and night, in continuous petitions and tears. Through His miraculous intercession today I was given ink and some paper with which to write you. Although you are absent from my eyes because of my sins, I always see you with the eyes of my soul and heart . . ., my injured orphan, gifted by God, by whose mercies you will be protected.

I was seized by my Lord's will for the well-being of my soul and accused by the good Lucena. You were apprehended on suspicion only; and if your innocence is doubted here, see in this a sign not of hatred but of the great love that God, our heavenly Father, has for you.

Rejoice and be happy, blessed daughter, that this is the road to paradise and to the glory that awaits you. Along this road have passed all the saints who now regale in it [glory]. Oh, what beautiful necklaces of pearl and opal the Lord will order to be placed on your injured neck, my martyr; oh, what beautiful chains of gold and what jewels in return for all that you have suffered. There, there, my innocent and patient one, I demand from you joy for the glory that awaits you. . . . There, my chaste girl, the wings of the Father of orphans will protect you, as they did Ruth. Fight, fight, against suffering and pain, as did the sainted Deborah, Judith, and Salome the blessed martyr, and you will be blessed by the Almighty.

There, there, beautiful one, enrich your soul, and, like Rachel, you will be loved; like Leah, you will be fertile in generating virtues; and, like Sarah you will be faithful. . . . Meditate and pray with Anna and Esther, and trust in God with blessed Susanna, that they will free you from false testimony. There, beloved, all the saints will dance in paradise at your wedding, when the Royal Sovereign of glory receives your soul as spouse. There, my Queen of Sheba, prepare yourself, for you will go to the holy city of Jerusalem of the heavens to see the beautiful King of angels, a King full of wisdom.

Oh, what beauties He will show you, what paradises, what orchards and gardens, what vineyards, what fruits; oh, what flowers, what fountains of perfumed waters, what hills covered with lilies; oh, what streams of milk and honey. There, pains and prison are just a road to all this. Take to the Lord, your Father, as a present from this debased earth, a bouquet made of all the flowers: those of patience, faith, hope, chastity, and obedience as a devout soul; for these are the flowers of paradise, flowers that never perish. Oh, what a wonderful odor these carnations have before God. He will repay you for present [woes] with eternal joy.

What beautiful attire He will have you wear, what skirts of beautiful silks, what blouses of cloth, cloth of rich brocade, what lovely gold-embroidered headdresses, what garlands of vivid flowers, what receptions and feasts and dances you will enjoy, what music played by holy cherubs and angels you will hear if you humble yourself before God and pray and have patience. For who with such hopes feels afflicted, who would not dance in prisons and jails. Joy, joy! Let anxiety and sighing cease, for the Lord has unveiled His great marvels to me; and to Him I commit you, my angels. May He visit you and save you, amen.

I am the Almighty's slave, though unworthy.

———◆———

In the original the following letters were not addressed to any specific person. When a name appears in the salutation, it has been inserted because of references that the letter contains or because of information obtained from other sources.

———◆———

Sequina upon us.

Blessed, may the Lord grant you good nights and days of salvation. If I am not mistaken, judging by your signs, I understand that your cell companion is either a Negress or a mulatto. If this is so, I am correct in my thoughts. May the Lord overlook all our faults, for he whose soul is always accompanied by thoughts of the good Creator need only wish that He be with him and with us all, amen. Your riddle made me laugh very much. May good riddles occur to you.

See, angel, in the beehive I saw that all the kingdoms and worldly goods, compared to the kingdom that our blessed and saintly God will grant us, are like one compared to sixty.

This sea of a prison leads us happily to a good port. In the kingdom of the Prince of peace women will painlessly bear their just children until their number is completed. Birds will come out at our call, and fish and beasts will obey our orders. The Lord will grant great glory to those who believe in Him and await Him, amen.

———◆———

[Written *ca.* summer 1595]

Blessed be God, Sequina, and may His highest presence be with you and all of you. You must know that His saintly mercy grants me many good things and favors here. Await Him and call Him, and subject yourselves to Him, and He will grant you mercy from His hand. He took me out of a dark cell in which I was locked for three weeks, blessed be His name. Now, day and night, I see the skies through a little window.

[115]

For eight days I had a honeycomb of the sweetest nectar from the Almighty's mouth. I ate from it, and my eyes were opened. I perceived great mysteries, and [I had] revelations of times to come and the freedom for which we hope. At the coming of Jacob's star all our dead will rise again to live and enjoy His kingdom. All those who had faith in God, from which stems the root of eternal life, all those whose hearts are filled with this knowledge, will be transplanted from this base earth. . . . I shall tell you now as much as the paper will allow.

Be comforted, my martyr, for we shall see each other soon. Pray that the Lord will open your eyes and that you will see hidden marvels, which are the sweets with which He regales His children. I saw that *ceci*[23] has four strands, each in turn folded, representing the four seasons of the year: summer, winter, autumn, and spring. The folded strands signify the days and nights of time, during which man must act, talk, and think constantly of the blessed law of God. These threads were crossed by five branches turned downward. Three of them had three knots each: the first signifying the three ages of the just: infancy, youth, and old age, during which we must all occupy ourselves in the [above-mentioned] blessed acts, ruminating like a clean animal on this perfumed and pungent anise.

The second branching strand with its three knots represents the three stages of the blessed law of nature written on the Holy Tablets and the coming of the Messiah, the true Christ, through the grace of the Lord, to our innermost beings and hearts. The other three branches signify the three ages of the synagogue, the Church of Almighty God, which is now old and must soon be renewed, for it is now 5346 [*sic*] years since God created the world. The other two knots signify the present and forthcoming centuries. This is the signal of the blessed children of God, of whom is sung, *Beatus vir*. Blessed and fortunate are the just. Blessed the tree that is planted on the edge of this river and that will forever be green, always having leaves, fruit, and flowers in summer, the time of fruitfulness, as well as in winter, the time of adversity. We must fight with patience, obedience, and prayer. Oh, how fragrant these carnations smell before the Lord. They will secure great mercies for you from Him, just as Noah's sacrifice did.

23. Possibly a corrupt form of *caelum*, the sky or heavens, or more likely of the Hebrew word *tizizit*, the garment with four fringes on it that the Jews were directed to wear. See Num. 15:37–41.

Hearken—when reciting the Shema, when you say, "Thou shalt love" [the Lord thy God], add "the ten holy commandments"; and then [add] the words, "I saw this your daughter imprisoned in jail." All these are God's revelations to me. Pray, pray, for ours is the living God and always will be.

———◆———

[To Catalina:]

My blessed one, the shield of the truth of the loving God will protect you and support you and your companions from temptation. As though it were so decreed, in this abyss God grants me the means of sending you a support, a staff[24] fashioned from the paradise of His Holy Scriptures, so that your weak spirit may be sustained and you may be better able to climb the steep hill of loneliness and imprisonment which leads to the summit of paradise and glory. This summit is what the Lord in His goodness offers to those souls who climb it with faith and patience, holding on to His holy compassion so as to achieve it. Take, then, this staff every day in the hand of your memory, so that you will not falter.

God tested Abraham and told him: "Abraham, Abraham, take your beloved son Isaac and sacrifice him to Me on one of the mountains that I shall indicate to you." Upon His divine command our holy father Abraham arose early, before sunrise, made his ass ready, and cut wood for the sacrifice. Then he took with him his son Isaac and two house servants and headed for Mount Moriah, where many years later the holy Temple was built, as the Lord had ordained. (Alas! May the Lord accompany us in the steps of our tribulation for the sake of those faithful footsteps of Abraham, amen.)

Upon arriving, Abraham said to his servants: "Remain at the foot of the mountain while we climb up to worship the Lord, after which we shall come down." He then placed the wood on his son's back, took a

24. Luis must have referred here to a prayer. *Baculo* can also be interpreted as a reference to Jacob's staff. It likewise has a metaphorical meaning of "relief" or "consolation."

knife and fire in his hands, and both went up together. Isaac . . . said to his father, "Father, I see that we have fire, wood, and a knife, but I do not see a victim for our sacrifice." Abraham replied, "The Lord will supply it, my son." (Just as He provided then and does provide in the greatest need, may the Lord provide now—for the love we bear You, O holy Father! Come to aid us in our travails and sorrows, amen.)

Upon arriving at the top of the mountain, Abraham said to his son: "My son, you have to know that the Lord our God has commanded me to offer you as a holy sacrifice to His Divine Majesty. Blessed and fortunate are you, since it is certain and without doubt that, among the sons of Adam, you [will be the first to] die in a royal manner as an offering to God, the almighty Lord of eternal life. I envy you rather than feel sorry for you, my son."

"You are offering me to the Lord," answered the holy Isaac (son of such a blessed father. O holy people, O holy conquerors of the kingdom of heaven which awaits us!), "Certainly, my father; if the Lord orders it this way, may His will be carried out, as I am here, obedient and prepared. Only, I beg of you, put a band across the eyes of this frail body, so that it may not see the knife when you deliver the blow and flee, for the spirit and the soul are obedient [but the flesh] is not to be denied."

Devotedly they embraced and wept as they took leave of each other. The father might have said, "Lord, for this Thou gavest me a son in my old age—to bestow this great affliction on me! It would have been better not to have given him to me." No, no, there was no sign of unfaithfulness in our saintly father, only his living faith in the Lord, who would fulfill the promises that had been made. If he sacrificed his son, God would renew [His promise]. In this manner Abraham took his son and tied his feet and hands. (Alas! for the sake of that saint thus bound and his faithful father, may our Lord give us patience and obedience to imitate them by offering ourselves to His holiness, amen.) He placed Isaac on top of the wood and the altar which he had arranged and lifted his hand to destroy him. How humbly the saint awaited his fate! When Abraham was about to deliver the blow, the Angel of the most blessed God called to him and checked his arm. He said to Abraham [using the direct words of God]: "Abraham, do not touch the child, as it is not My will that Isaac should die, but rather [it is My will] to give you My eternal glory and reward." Courage,

courage, my imprisoned ones; God does not want your death, but wants to give you eternal and true life through this˙experience.

The Angel said: "You have shown Me how much you love Me, since you did not hesitate to spare your own son. Since you acted in such a manner, you will be requited handsomely." How insignificant are our accomplishments compared to the greatness of the reward and the glory that the Lord promises and grants us, provided we have faith in Him.

Abraham saw a ram caught in the bushes which the Lord had provided. After he offered it, the Lord's Angel called to Abraham a second time [and said]: " 'I promised Myself,' said the Lord, 'that if you did not spare the son whom I gave you with My love, I would return him to you and [give you] as many more children as there are stars and grains of sand. Your seed [descendants] will possess the gates of their enemies, and from your seed will come the true Messiah in Christ. All the people of the earth will be blessed through you and will thereby come unto Me.' " Abraham prayed with reverence to the Lord, and then with great joy father and son returned to their home.

Lo! lo! my martyrs, have faith in the midst of temptation, and you will not die. Remember, my souls, that while the saintly Abraham was tying his son, the Angel of the Lord was providing the ram that was offered in his son's place. Kneel before God and ask for His hand and help, which He will then offer us. Because of His great mercy He always rescues His own in moments of greatest danger. May He come to you, amen.

[To Mariana:]

May Adonai protect you and me. You will live, you will live, my lost ones, my languid ones; happy, happy blessed martyrs of the living God, who will visit you in His mercy.

Through His intercession there has come to my hand today ink and this bit of paper, so that I am able to write to you. Although I am deprived of the sight of you and your sweet company because of my sins, I have [a vision of] you always before my eyes. There are many brief periods when my tears gush forth like a torrent of water for your afflictions. Then there are other times when my heart is full of pleasure because the Almighty opens my eyes to show me that this is the right road to glory and that only His kindness can lead you to Him. To the right and left of us there is always danger of fire and deep water, as you have heard in [the books of] Esdras.

Let us not stray from Him with lack of faith and patience, but let us give infinite thanks to our Lord because of the attention paid to us miserable worms. He tests us as He tested our saints. Only as regards myself have I confessed His [the Lord's] truth, not wishing to utter false testimony against anyone. It is this truth that is my strong shield while I am in prisons and in chains, with which I await the day of my glory. Then with His help I shall see myself at the feet of the Lord.

Your arrest was based on suspicion only. Now we can clearly see that it was the will of the Almighty to take you to His paradise and glory by way of these prisons without further detours or the distractions of Castile, where we were to go. The change in our plans is a change for the better rather than a denial of our wishes, even though in the middle of the road there is this uphill path through this prison and our loneliness. Since we have the divine promises to sustain us in our climb, let no one be discouraged.

When you feel tired and worn out, as has happened with me, you should kneel in heart and body and ask the Almighty for help, and He will grant it. Through the prophet Isaiah He promised to take the tired and wounded unto Himself. His holiness dwells eternally in His sanctuary and exists for the sake of the afflicted and humble ones, whose hearts will be revived and whose spirits will be cheered. "I Myself," He says, "shall console them. I shall have mercy on My poor, frightened children. Heaven is the seat of My glory, and the vast earth is My footstool. My eyes will search for the wounded ones who have been humiliated and worried, fearing My word" [judgments].

He further says, "Do not fear, My children, children of Abraham, My friend and children of My chosen Israel, in whose hearts is the holy law. Do not fear the hatred of men and their blasphemies because, like a cloak, they will be eaten by the worms; and, just as moths eat wool, they will be destroyed. My eternal salvation will rest upon you. The heavens will vanish like smoke, and the earth will become old and will be discarded like a worn cloth, but the salvation that I promise will never be lacking and will be eternally with you."

This is said by Him who created the laws that rule the heavens, the nights, and the days; whose hand dried the sea [Red Sea] and the waters of the abyss and made the path through which His [people] could walk to liberation. Be happy and be in high spirits, and leap for joy like little well-fed lambs. He promised to save us and to fill us with eternal joy and happiness. He will make beautiful crowns, putting them on the heads of His beloved little children who believe in Him and await Him and are fearful of Him.

Console yourselves, my blessed martyrs, for you go like queens, like Sarah, from this base and woeful earth to see the King of angels, who rules heaven and earth with glory and with great wisdom. You are going to see the rich, holy palaces, the orchards of paradise, the garden wherein is the Tree of Life, the vineyards of muscatel, the roses, the fruit-bearing trees, and the brooklets of milk and honey. . . . Your loving Father [God], who brought you to this world, will embrace you and give you His blessing. Oh, how He will take from his pockets the handkerchief of consolation. With gifts He will wipe away your tears. He will tell you that there will be no further tribulations. He will embrace you as does a loving mother who enfolds her son in her arms when he says something humorous. She gives him a thousand hugs and kisses, and desires to have him return within her body.

He will embrace you and say, "Come to Me, My little ones, you who have suffered so much for My honor and My law." He will have you wear clothes of heavy brocade and coifs made of fine gold; chains, jewels, rings, and crowns of laurels such as are worn by conquerors. What dancing and what a festival there will be on the day of your nuptials! How we shall dance and sing with joy! The holy David will play the harp so that we may dance with the angels and saints, who await us with great happiness. He [God] blesses and cheers those who do not fear prisons, death, and fire.

Be consoled, and have consolation in [the ultimate] victory. Be suffused with high spirits and gladness like Asenecs in their penitential prayer, like Annas and Esthers; be like beautiful Rachels, faithful Sarahs, pure Susannas, strong Jaels and Judiths and blessed Salomes. Sing a song of victory with Deborah and Mary.[25]

25. Deborah and Miriam were two Jewish women who sang famous songs of victory. Deborah's canticle is to be found in Judges, chap. 5. Miriam's song follows that of Moses in Exod. 15:20–21.

the last will and testament

OF

JOSEPH LUMBROSO

[Luis de Carvajal, *el Mozo*]

One experiences a very strange sensation as he runs over the lines traced by the hands of those unfortunate ones who, surrounded by enemies and traitors and expecting soon to perish by bonfire, still showed such ardent faith and such sublime rectitude of soul.

—GENERAL VICENTE RIVA PALACIO, *México a traves de los siglos* [*1867*]

Fig. 13: Official seal of the Tribunal of the Holy Office
of the Mexican Inquisition

testament of
luis de carvajal

IN WHICH HE SAID HE WISHES TO DIE

 HIGHEST AND ALMIGHTY God of heaven and earth, whose will none of the things Thou hast created can resist, and without whose will men, fowl, beasts, and animals could not live on earth: If Thy will did not provide and maintain order in the elements, heaven would be confounded and all things would lose their course and natural movements. The earth would tremble, the peaks and great hills would fall, the waters of the sea would cover the earth, and no living thing would be maintained. Thou, by Thine infinite kindness and mercy, dost order and sustain all, not because it is necessary to Thee but for the general benefit and profit of mankind. And because Thou bestowest so much kindness and infinite mercy upon all [men], I, the poorest and most miserable of all, beg and implore in charity that Thou, in the impending moments of my death, which I wish to welcome in honor of Thy holy name and genuine law, mayest not forsake me. Accept in Thy mercy this poor life that Thou gavest me, not looking at my innumerable sins and this immortal soul, which Thou didst create in Thine image for eternal life. I beg Thee to forgive and receive it when it leaves this mortal body. Putting in order my testament, my final and ultimate will, . . . I write and sign the religious truths in which I believe and which I reaffirm [before I] die in Thy presence.

[125]

First: I believe in the one and only God, almighty and true, Creator of heaven, earth and sea, and of all the visible and invisible things; and I renounce the devil and all his lies.

Second: I believe that God our Lord and universal Creator, is one and no more. Deuteronomy 4: "Hear, O Israel, the Lord thy God, is one, and there is no other." He is the God of the heavens above and the earth below. Deut. 32: *Confirmatur videte quod ego sum solq.* etc.[1]

Third: I believe that the law of God our Lord, which the Christians call the dead law of Moses, is alive and everlasting, as recorded in the holy Pentateuch. Therein God attested to it in a thousand places, *Ego Dns.* etc., saying and ordering that it be observed in *Sempiternas generationes,* that is, forever and ever. Likewise blessed David testified (Psalm 110) where he said, "True are all His commandments, confirmed forever, endlessly made according to truth and equality," etc.;[2] *ibi mandauit in eternum testamentum suu,*[3] etc.; and [the same occurs] in many other places, e.g., Malachai, *Ego Dns. etnomutur.*[4] *Nume non es homo deg ut mutetur ps⁰ cogitationes cordie eig,* etc. *ps⁰ Salmo 118 pertotum . . .*[5]

What Christians say about the ceremonials and Judaic precepts being dead and having expired is against one of their own Gospels, which says, *"noliteputare, etc."*[6]; for really and certainly *facilius est coelis et terra transfire quan iota unum autapex alegeperire.*[7] It is a great

1. "Videte quod ego sim solus, et non sit alius Deus praeter me" (Deut. 32:39, Vulg.); "See now that I, even I, am He, And there is no god with Me; . . ." (JPS).

2. ". . . All His precepts are sure. They are established for ever and ever, They are done in truth and uprightness." (Ps. 111:7–8, JPS). This Psalm bears the number 111 in Hebrew editions of the Old Testament and in most vernacular versions. Luis, however, gave the reference as Psalm 110, since he had been trained in the use of the Vulgate Bible, which has a slight difference from the Hebrew version in the numbering of most of the psalms.

3. "Mandavit in aeternum testamentum suum" (Ps. 110:9, Vulg.); ". . . He hath commanded His covenant for ever;" (Ps. 111:9, JPS).

4. "Ego enim Dominus, et mutor" (Mal. 3:6, Vulg.); "For I the Lord change not; . . . " (JPS).

5. Usually numbered Psalm 119 in vernacular versions.

6. "Nolite putare quoniam veni solvere legem, aut prophetas" (Matt. 5:17, Vulg.); "Think not that I am come to destroy the law or the prophets: . . ." (R.V.).

7. "Amen quippe dico vobis, donec transeat coelum et terra, iota unum, aut unus apex non praeteribit a lege, donec omnia fiant" (Matt. 5:18, Vulg.); "For verily I say unto you, Till heaven and earth pass, one jot or one tittle shall in no wise pass from the law, till all be fulfilled." (R.V.).

temerity on the part of man to wish to change the Commandments of God our Lord; this is a dishonor to the Legislator: *constant Eccls. ibi Non posumus eis sadere nec ausenequid qz.,* etc.[8] We cannot add or take away anything, and this is the express order of our Lord in Deuteronomy: *ibi-Nonades adverbum,* etc.[9]

The *fourth* belief of mine is that it is a sin to worship idols and images, because it is against the Commandments of God our Lord: Exod. & Deut. 6-0-7[10]—*ibi Nonfaciestibi sculptile aut aliqud similitudinen,* etc. *Confirmatum Jerem 10, ibi opus risidignum,* etc., *Isac ibi corinsi piens adorabitil,* etc. *Non recogitate,* etc. *Item salmo 112 ibi simulachra gentium,* etc. *Alibim confundantur omnes,* etc., *omnes gentium dem⁰,* etc.;[11] and that which the Christians say against this is heretical. And if I should be inclined to believe it, may God reprove me strongly, for He has already advised me of what I should believe: *Inmolauerum doemoniis, et non Deo diis ignorabant,* etc.;[12] and . . . Deut.: "There shall be no man or woman among you whose heart shall part from our Lord and be the root which generates bile and bitterness, and [who shall] make or adore any idols, for the ire and

---

8. "Non possumus eis quidquan addere, nec auferre, quae fecit Deus ut timeatur" (Eccles. 3:14, Vulg.); ". . . nothing can be added to it, nor anything taken from it; and God hath so made it, that men should fear before him." (JPS).

9. "Non addetis ad verbum, quod vobis loquor, nec auferetis ex eo" (Deut. 4:2, Vulg.); "Ye shall not add unto the word which I command you, neither shall ye diminish from it, . . ." (JPS).

10. Luis' references are incomplete here. Deut., chap. 6, is concerned with the Commandments; Exod., chap. 7, is not.

11. "Non facies tibi sculptile, nec similitudinem omnium, quae in coelo sunt desuper" (Deut. 5:8, Vulg.); "Thou shalt not make unto thee a graven image, the likeness of any form that is in the heaven above, . . ." (R.V.).

"Vana sunt, et opus risu dignum" (Jer. 10:15, Vulg.); "They are vanity, a work of delusion; . . ." (JPS).

"Cor insipiens adoravit illud, et non liberabit animan suam" (Isa. 44:20, Vulg.); ". . . A deceived heart hath turned him aside, That he cannot deliver his soul, . . ." (JPS).

". . . simulacra gentium" (Ps. 112:4, Vulg.); "Their idols are silver and gold, . . ." (Ps. 115:4, JPS).

"Confundantur omnes qui adorant sculptilia" (Ps. 97:7, Vulg.); "Ashamed be all they that serve graven images, . . ." (JPS).

12. "Immolaverunt daemoniis et non Deo, diis, quod ignorabant" (Deut. 32:17, Vulg.); "They sacrificed unto demons which were no God, to gods whom they knew not, . . ." (R.V.).

fury of the Lord will grow," etc.[13] Further, I say that if a man with the figure of an angel of light should tell me that the keeping of the holy Sabbath, so stressed and sternly ordered in so many parts of the law of our Lord God, had ceased, and that it is no longer a sin to eat blood, suet, and pork, something which is not only against the written laws but against the natural laws, I would not believe him either, even if he should also tell me sacred things; [but I would persevere] . . . firmly in the faith of the true word of the Lord, as His Divine Majesty advises and orders me. Deut. 13: *ibi—Si surregerite,* etc., *pertotum.*[14]

[There is no Number 5.]

Sixth: I believe that the Sacred Sacrament of Circumcision is eternal, as God our Lord said to the holy Abraham and then to the holy Moses: "The soul of the man that will not be circumcized will be erased from the list of living" (Gen. 17).[15]

Seventh: I believe that Christ,[16] the true Father of the future son, Prince of peace, real son of David, possessor of the scepter of Judah . . . has not arrived [and] that the redemption of the people and world of God has not been achieved, since it is clearly established by all the sacred prophets and particularly by chapter 39 of Ezekiel that by the good grace of God our Lord, all dead [who were] faithful to Israel will be revived, and all dispersed and living Jews [will be] congregated from all parts of the earth:[17] Jeremiah-*ibi-Non-dicetur ultra vivit Dns.,* etc.[18] through even greater miracles than those performed by the Lord when He rescued us from Egypt. Neither the glorious Jerusalem nor the marvelous Temple of God, which is to last

13. See Deut. 29:16–17: "And ye have seen their abominations, and their idols, wood and stone, silver and gold, which were among them: lest there be among you man, or woman, or family, or tribe, whose heart turneth away this day from the Lord our God, to go to serve the gods of those nations; lest there should be among you a root that beareth gall and wormwood;" (R.V.).

14. "Si surrexerit in medio tui prophetas . . ." (Deut. 13:2, Vulg.); "If there arise in the midst of thee a prophet, . . ." (JPS).

15. "And the uncircumcised male who is not circumcised in the flesh of his fore-skin, that soul shall be cut off from his people; he hath broken My covenant.'" (Gen. 17:14, JPS).

16. He uses the name of Christ in its literal meaning—Messiah.

17. Luis erred in giving the number of the chapter. This is apparently a sum-marizing statement of the contents of Ezek. 37:1–14, in which the prophet's vision of the Valley of Dry Bones is revealed.

18. "Non dicetur ultra: Vivit Dominus, qui eduxit filios Israel de terra Aegypti" (Jer. 16:14, Vulg.); ". . . it shall no more be said: 'As the Lord liveth that brought up the children of Israel out of the land of Egypt,'" (JPS).

for all ages, have been rebuilt, as prophesied by Isaiah and Job. *Aggaeo* [Haggai]. *Ad huepusillum,* etc.; and never again shall Israel be enslaved. *Thren. Non adii ciet ut transmigret te ultra. Baruch. Non conmouebo amplius filius, Israel a terra quan dabo illis,* etc.;[19] wars will cease as well as the sins and idolatries of the world (Isaiah, David, Daniel and Ezekiel); all men shall be converted to the knowledge of the true God and man restored to his first stage of innocence (Isaiah and Micah, Joel and Abadiah). Finally, it is clear from a reading of the Prophets and in almost every one of their chapters and in almost all of their statements that it is the benighted blind who deserve to prove that the snow is not white and that there are no nights, only days. May the infinite God, for whom it is [possible], grieve for those who live in total darkness and may He place them on the road to His light, amen.

Eighth: I believe in what relates to the mysterious vision of the holy Daniel, since I have been accused of that belief in this proceso. I believe that the three beasts which the lion first saw were: the Chaldean Empire, which was cruel and fierce to the Church of God our Lord, that is, His beloved people Israel; the eye, the Persians and Medes, less fierce to her [Israel], because with them was Cyrus, called Christ by Isaiah, that is, consecrated by God, in whose time our Lord freed His people from the Babylonian captivity; and the linnet, with its wings and varied colors, that is, the empire of the Greeks and of Alexander with his conquests and various victories. Thus the fourth beast, frightful and fiercest of them all, which bit all with its teeth and trampled on everything with its feet, prefigured this fourth monarchy, which endures until this very day, as is clearly stated in the words of the angel Saint Gabriel, who showed the prophet Daniel the ten horns—these being the ten kings who ruled until, from among them, on the head of the same beast, sprang up the small horn with two eyes and one mouth that uttered great blasphemies against God the Exalted One.[20]

[To attribute] passion to God is impossible; and since He is One, to

19. "Non addet ultra ut transmigret te" (Lam. 4:22, Vulg.); ". . . He will no more carry thee away into captivity; . . ." (JPS).

". . . et non mouebo amplius populum meum filios Israel a terra quam dedi illis" (Bar. 2:35, Vulg.); ". . . and I will no more remove My people, the children of Israel, out of the land that I have given them." (D.V.).

20. See Dan. chap. 7.

say that He is three and that God's law is dead, that the infinite is finite, the eternal only temporal, that the cause is the effect, and that the Lord is a slave, and that God is a man . . . is impossible, in addition to being against the teachings of the law of God. . . . The Lord states (in Joel): *congregato omnes gentes in valle Josaphat et ibi,* etc.; "and I will judge them for the harm they did to My people";[21] and in chapters 49 and 66 of Isaiah: *ibi-igniseo non extinguetur,*[22] because they loved and chose all that God forbade and abhorred. And then the kingdom will be restored to Christ and to the saints of the sublime God: *Dan-ibi-Conbalecebat cun nubg coeli,*[23] etc. . . .

◆

[Here follows a passage that is quite obscure, and a tortuous comparison is made, so that I doubt whether Luis fully expressed his thought in this section. He then uses as an analogy (1) the dream of Nebuchadnezzar, which Daniel, through a vision from God, was able to interpret (Daniel 2: 31–45); and (2) the present divisions of nations, all of which will ultimately fall. The only kingdom that will survive, writes Luis, is that of God, and God alone will create this kingdom. The allegory and references stem from the section of Daniel cited above.]

◆

The stone that fell on the statue [seen by Nebuchadnezzar in his dream] without being pushed, as the king saw in his dream, destroyed it. [The statue symbolized the empire of Babylon.] It was destroyed because it stood on a foundation of iron and clay, a very poor combination or mixture. These divisions [poor mixtures] are seen [today] as divisions among heretical [nations], such as the English, the French,

21. "Congregabo omnes Gentes et deducam eas in vallem Josaphat: et disceptabo cum eis ibi super populo meo, et hereditate mea Israel" (Joel 4:2, Vulg.); "I will gather all nations, And will bring them down into the valley of Jehoshaphat; And I will enter into judgment with them there for My people and for My heritage Israel, . . ." (JPS).

22. "Et Ignis eorum non extinguetur" (Isa. 66:24, Vulg.); ". . . Neither shall their fire be quenched; . . ." (JPS).

23. "Et ecce cum nubibus coeli quasi filius hominis veniebat" (Dan. 7:13, Vulg.); ". . . and, behold, one like the Son of Man came with the clouds of heaven, . . .' (R.V.)

and others who used to be the feet of that statue; but no longer do they mix well. This signalizes the great fall that they will suffer [because they do not acknowledge the primacy of the one God, and their stress is on the temporal]: *Constatetian,* Deut. 32: *ibi de vite, sedon,* etc. *usque ego retribuan ei sinten pore quo lebatur peseo.*[24]

[There is no Number 9.]

Tenth: I believe that King Antiochus,[25] whom the Holy Scriptures called root of sin because he was the persecutor of God's people and of His holy law, represents the kings of Spain and Portugal. They have been and still are the root from which originate the branches of the inquisitions and the persecutions of the people of God and His holy law and of the blessed martyrs who are the faithful and true Jews and who die for their faith in this law. The princes who persecute call them judaizing heretics. However, judaizing is not heresy but is living according to the Commandments of God our Lord. . . .

Moreover, I confess and declare that if I consented to have theologians[26] and sly men come twice, it was not because I ever doubted these certain and complete truths (for I believe in them more than in my manhood) but in order to discuss them widely, and *urta illub Thob-ult°.*[27] Confess to the Lord, you sons of Israel, and praise Him before men, because for that purpose you were placed among them by Him: so that you can tell all strangers about His wonders and let them know that there is no other God, omnipotent and true, but Him, etc. Also, I tried if possible to convert them [the theologians] and the

24. Chapter 32 of Deuteronomy is the Song of Moses. Luis seems to be quoting from verse 35: "Mea est ultio, et ego retribuam in tempore, ut labatur pes eorum: juxta est dies perditionis, et adesse festinant tempora" (Vulg.); "Vengeance is Mine, and recompense, Against the time when their foot shall slip; for the day of their calamity is at hand, And the things that are to come upon them shall make haste." (JPS).

25. King Antiochus, who is called in I Macc. 1:11 "a wicked root" (D.V.). The kingdom of Judea was part of his territory by virtue of conquest. He decreed that the Jews who were his vassals should sacrifice to idols and desecrate the Sabbath. His actions led to the Maccabean revolt of 168 B.C.

26. At one of his hearings, after Luis had given a lengthy declamation of his beliefs, of Maimonides' Creed, and the reasons why he believed Christ not to be the Messiah, the inquisitors asked him whether he would permit two doctors of theology to discuss his beliefs with him. He consented.

27. Possibly intended as a reference to the last chapter in Tobias.

inquisitor princes, since they have showed me much affection and wished for my salvation. . . .

I again swear, in the name of the Almighty, to live and die for His faith. May it please Him, so that, imitating the zeal of Hananiah, Azariah, Mishael,[28] and Matathias,[29] I shall joyfully give away my soul for the faith of the Holy Testament for which they died—*Et siomnes obediant*,[30] etc.—and for the holy truths that are as clear as our Lord Himself spoke them in the canticle He taught to Moses: *Audite coeli*, etc.[31] . . . So I desire, and it is my wish to die for His holy faith and true law. I hope for strength from the Lord. I do not trust myself, since I am only flesh and of frail nature; and just as I have placed a mother and five sisters in danger for this faith, I would give away a thousand, if I had them, for the faith of each of His holy Commandments.

In testimony of which I wrote and signed this my will, and I conclude with this final answer (maintaining and reaffirming my faith) to the charges against me [by the Inquisition prosecutor]. My Lord, look upon me with grace, so that it may be known and seen in this kingdom and upon all the earth that Thou art our God and that Thine almighty and holy name, Adonai, is invoked with truth in Israel and among Israel's descendants. I commit this soul that Thou gavest me to Thy holy hands, promising with Thy help not to change my faith till death nor after it.

I end happily the narrative of my present life, having lively faith in Thy divine hope of saving me through Thine infinite mercy and of resurrecting me, when Thy holy will is accomplished, together with our fathers Abraham, Isaac, and Jacob and his faithful sons, for whose holy love I beg Thee humbly to confirm this and not to forsake me.

28. Hananiah, Azariah, and Mishael (Dan. 1:6–7; 3:8–25), captives of King Nebuchadnezzar, were of the tribe of Judah. Their names were changed to Shadrach, Abed-nego, and Meshach, respectively. In captivity they held to Jewish dietary laws and refused to eat the king's food. Ultimately, upon refusing to adore idols, they were cast into a fiery furnace, but they were not even singed and were permitted to leave the furnace unharmed.

29. Matathias was the Maccabean hero who defied the decree of King Antiochus to sacrifice to idols. (See I Macc. ch. 2). For three years (168–165 B.C.) he and his sons led the revolt which ended in liberation from Syrian rule.

30. Cf. Deut. 11:26–27; 28:1–14.

31. This is the opening of the Song of Moses (Deut. 32:1): "Give ear, ye heavens, and I will speak; And let the earth hear the words of my mouth." (JPS).

May it please Thee to send the angel Michael, our prince, to defend and help me with his holy and angelic host, and to aid me to persevere in, and die for, Thy holy faith, delivering me from the hands and temptations of the enemy. O Lord have mercy on the glory of Thy name, Thy law, and Thy people, and the world which Thou Thyself didst create; fill it [the world] with Thy light and the truthful knowledge of Thy name, so that heaven and earth will be filled with Thy glory and praise, amen, amen. Dated in Purgatory, the fifth month of the year five thousand three hundred and fifty-seven of our creation.

INQUISITOR'S NOTE:

Testament of Joseph Lumbroso, and the final answer he gives, thus definitely concluding his case.

epilogue

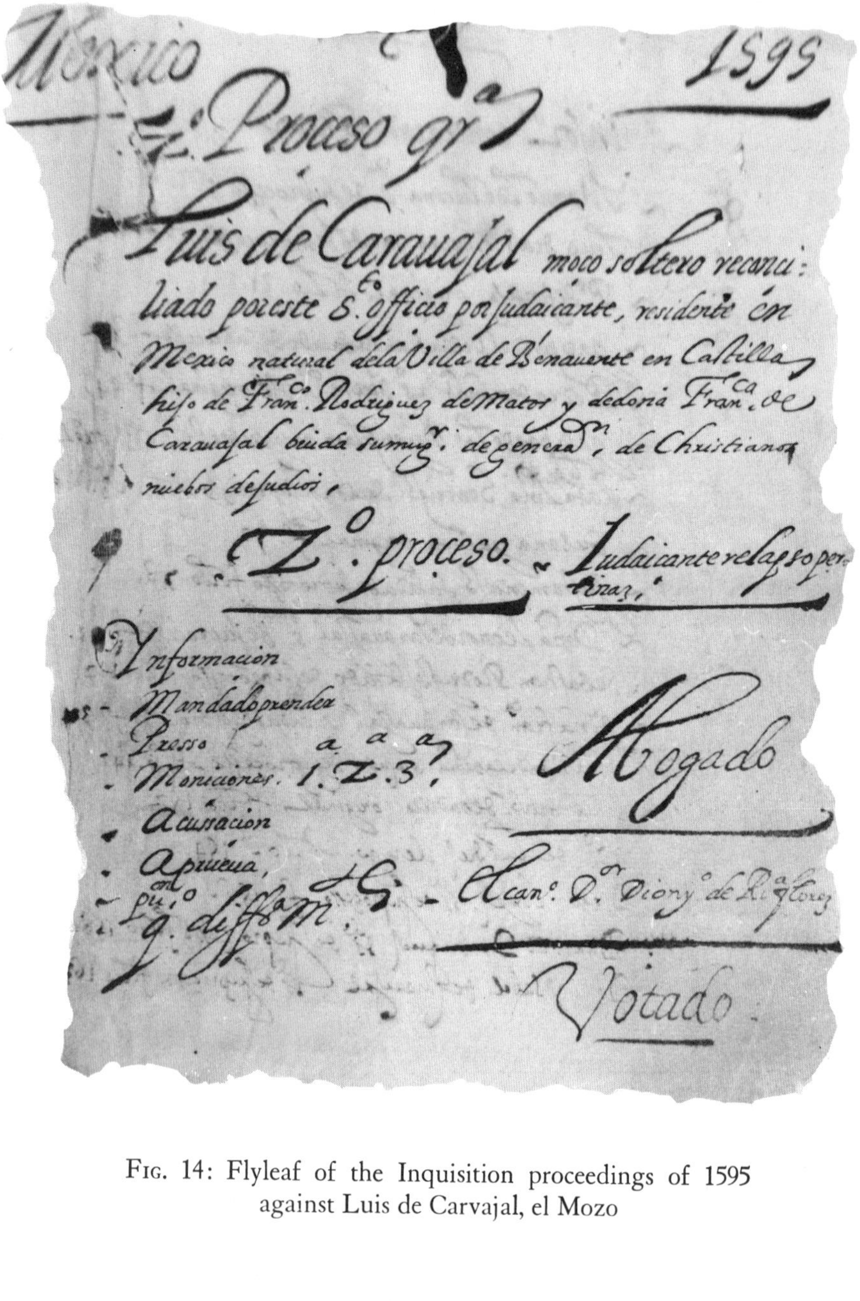

FIG. 14: Flyleaf of the Inquisition proceedings of 1595
against Luis de Carvajal, el Mozo

epilogue

———◦——————

THE STORY OF THE CARVAJAL FAMILY did not terminate with the tragic deaths of the immediate children of Francisco Rodríguez de Matos and Francisca Núñez de Carvajal. The Inquisition section of the Mexican National Archives has records dated as recently as 1706 concerning grandchildren, great-grandchildren, and great-great-grandchildren. Despite the known history of the family, rumors and reverberations were set in motion during this century which were supposedly extensions of the Carvajal story but which actually are mythical and an attempt to foster a legend.

About 1935 the spokesman of a small group of mestizos not far from Mexico City proclaimed that this people were descendants of the Carvajals. The claim was accepted without further investigation. Within a comparatively short time American Yiddish journalists and an American rabbi declared that there were "Indian Jews" in Mexico who were descendants of crypto-Jews who had resided in New Spain prior to 1821. These "Indian Jews" reportedly told gullible Americans that the Carvajals had intermarried with Indian women and that ever since the end of the sixteenth century they and their descendants had lived secretly in Indian villages. These people stated that they had not known of the existence of other Jews in Mexico until the mid-1930's, when they themselves were "discovered" by Rabbi Morris Clark. In 1956, this rabbi retracted his statements and said that the Jewishness of the Indian Mexican Jews was of recent genesis.[1]

1. See the letter of Rabbi Morris Clark in Joseph Gumbiner's "The Indian Jews of Mexico," *American Judaism,* V (January, 1956), p. 11.

Printed accounts of the survival of the group vary with each narrator. Like quicksilver, details were elusive and were supplanted by vague generalities. Those who interested themselves in the group were not very familiar with Mexican history and were unaware that these people had formerly belonged to a Christian Sabbatarian sect, the *Iglesia de Dios* (Church of God). The inquirers lacked knowledge of the dogma of this sect and were insensitive to the psychology of the Mexican. Thus, imaginative accounts were accepted as true. The art of questioning, deftly and subtly employed, often reveals what Carl L. Becker so aptly stated: "Passionate faith and expert rationalism are apt to be united." He continued, "It is not always possible to press what William James called 'the irreducible brute facts' into the neat categories of faith."[2]

Since no one bothered to ascertain the facts, the legend spread in English-speaking countries. It had short shrift in Mexico because the official rabbinate of the various Jewish groups, Sephardim, Ashkenazim, and Oriental, held that these people were not Jews. However, few outsiders inquired of Mexican Jews, and many of those who did and were informed then chose to disregard what they had learned. It is trite but true that people believe what they want to believe, especially when an exotic or esoteric element is present.

In brief, the salient portion of the story dispensed by the "Indian Jews" is that they are descendants of the Carvajals and of some of their friends; and that during the last decade of the sixteenth century some of the Carvajal family and other Jews had sought refuge from the Inquisition in Indian villages, where they secreted themselves. There they intermarried with Indian women and reared families and passed on from generation to generation the legacy of their ancestry. The modern mestizos, self-proclaimed descendants of the colonial Jews, assert that there were no other Jews but themselves in colonial Mexico after 1600 and say that they finally "came out of hiding" about 1910.

They apparently do not know that ever since the *Leyes de Reforma* of Juarez in 1857 freedom of religion has been firmly established in Mexico; that Jews have been living in the country without interruption ever since 1521; and that there were secret synagogues in Mexico City, Guadalajara, Veracruz, and other places in the mid-seventeenth cen-

2. Carl L. Becker, *The Heavenly City of the Eighteenth Century Philosophers* (New Haven: 1932), pp. 8, 9.

tury. These and many other historical facts impeach the esoteric tale. Of course, the mestizos did not consider that their connection with and membership in Christian sects might be disclosed. However, it has been established that prior to their adoption of Judaism they had been led from Catholicism to membership in a Christian Sabbatarian sect.

Actually, Judaism as a formal, institutionalized faith cannot be unilaterally adopted.[3] According to Jewish law, the mestizos are not Jews. The orthodox, traditional law prescribes that only a child born of a Jewish mother or a person who has converted in a formal manner before a religious body can be considered a Jew. Even modern extreme Reform definitions include the necessity of acceptance as a Jew by the local Jewish community. The acceptance as Jews is nonexistent in this case.

Confusion for uninformed American tourists resulted from the use of the word *Israelita*. The Jews of contemporary Latin America are known as *Israelitas* rather than as *Judíos*. The two words are synonymous. The disciples of the Iglesia de Dios, claiming to be descendants of the biblical Jacob, Isaac's son who was given the name Israel when he wrestled with an angel,[4] also term themselves *Israelitas*. In the Mexican government decennial census they register under the category *Israelita,* which follows that of *Católico* and *Protestante*.

Two anthropologists who have studied the largest community of "Indian Jews" (about fifty) in Venta Prieta, have stated that the group is beginning to admit that their claim to Jewish ancestry is a myth.[5] Among those at Venta Prieta there had always been some elders who had labeled as fiction the tale told by members of their own families. These elders asserted that their people had been of the Catholic faith until the end of the nineteenth century and had then converted to the Iglesia de Dios, whose dogma includes belief in Jesus as one of the Trinity and as the Messiah, veneration of Mary, who immaculately conceived Him, and many of the doctrines of Catholicism. Some of the variances from Catholicism include the fixing of the Sabbath for

3. See Salo Wittmayer Baron, *History and Jewish Historians* (Philadelphia: 1964), pp. 20, 21; and Jacob R. Marcus, *American Jewish Archives,* XVII (April, 1965), p. 17. Both authors cited are ordained Reform rabbis as well as noted historians.

4. See Gen. 32:24–30.

5. See Raphael Patai, "Venta Prieta Revisited," *Midstream,* XI (March, 1965), pp. 79–92. See also Seymour B. Liebman, "Mexican Mestizo Jews," *American Jewish Archives,* XIX (November, 1967).

Friday sundown to Saturday sunset, the observance of the Lord's Supper in accordance with the Hebrew lunar calendar on the same night as the commencement of the Jewish Passover, and refraining from eating pork products. After abandoning the Iglesia de Dios, these people began to call themselves members of the Jewish faith. In addition to professing belief in the biblical Mosaic laws, they have adopted many other Jewish practices. They yearn for tradition.

While the history of the true descendants of the Carvajals does not include the glamour of three hundred years of secret existence in Indian villages, and while the records of the family extend only to 1706, there are circumstances and events in the period between 1595 and 1706 which are of interest.

After 1601 the only two lineal descendants of Francisco Rodríguez de Matos and Francisca de Carvajal in Mexico were Anica de Carvajal, daughter, and Leonor de Cáceres, granddaughter. They were teenagers with a five-or-six year differential in their ages. Anica was about nineteen and Leonor about thirteen when both were reconciled in the auto-da-fé of March 25, 1601 and were given their freedom, although their sentences called for imprisonment.[6] Both saw Mariana de Carvajal, their sister and aunt, respectively, burned at the stake in 1601. Antonio Díaz de Cáceres, brother-in-law of Anica and father of Leonor, was also sentenced in the same auto-da-fé. He was fined a thousand duros of Castile, abjured *de vehementi,* and was to be exiled to Spain. He passes from the scene, and there is no further record of his presence nor proof that he left Mexico.

After March 25, 1601, Anica and Leonor, who had for a time lived in the same household, were separated by order of the Inquisiton. There seems to have been some animus on the part of Leonor against Anica for a time. Anica, who became known as Ana de León Carvajal, married a Portuguese Jew, Cristóbal Miguel. He died many years prior to 1642. They had a daughter, María de León. About 1629 María married Diego Núñez Pacheco, a Portuguese Jew. This couple had four

6. See Mexican Inquisition Documents bequeathed by Mr. Walter Douglas, Vol. II, *"Abecedario" of All Prisoners, 1528 to the Eighteenth Century,* at the Huntington Library. See also Seymour B. Liebman, "The Abecedario and a Check-List of Mexican Inquisition Documents in the Henry E. Huntington Library," *Hispanic American Historical Review,* XLIV (1964), pp. 554–567.

children: Luis, born in 1631; Manuel, born in 1635; Beatriz, in 1636; and Cristóbal, in 1641.[7] They lived in the small town or village of Cretano.

Diego Núñez Pacheco, María's husband, was arrested by the Holy Office in October, 1642 when he was fifty years of age.[8] Diego had come to New Spain in 1617. He was a traveling merchant, who traded in Texcoco, Pachuca, Zimapán, Cretano, Celaya, and at the mines of San Luis, Zacatecas, Guadalajara, and Guadiana, among other places. (These towns were the loci of Jewish settlements in the middle of the seventeenth century. During this era the word "Portuguese" was equated in New Spain with the term judío.) Diego Núñez died in his cell on May 12, 1643, without having admitted any of the charges against him. His mother-in-law, who was in another cell at the time, was informed of his demise.

Neither María de León nor any of her children were arrested during the era from 1642 to 1649, when more than four hundred Jews were sought by the Holy Office. María had been questioned in 1632 and liberated, as were several other Jews. During 1642 and 1643, after her husband was arrested, she had again been implicated by several prisoners of the Inquisition. There is no explanation for the failure to apprehend María during this period except that in the tremendous overload of pending matters before the Tribunal her case may have been overlooked. If an order of arrest had been issued and the constable not been able to locate her, that fact would have been recorded.

From the time she was arrested in 1643 until she went to the stake in 1649, María's mother, Anica de Carvajal, withstood all attempts of the inquisitors to have her reveal the identity of other Jews. During the six years she was in her cell she fasted, prayed, and observed as much Jewish ritual as she could. Inquisition eavesdroppers were kept outside the cell that she shared with another Jewess in the expectation of hearing names mentioned in their conversation. They reported that Anica constantly invoked Adonai and that her conversation concerned

7. Among the Spanish Jews of the time there was no custom of bestowing a given name of a deceased person to a new born child. The naming of the first child after the great-uncle, Luis the Younger, and another after his deceased grandfather, Cristóbal, were especially thoughtful and deliberate acts. The names as here given are to be found in Mexican Inquisition Documents, Vol. II, *ibid.*

8. Mexican National Archives, Inquisition Section, Tomo 382 (1642), Expediente 21.

places where she had prayed or studied in the past, i.e., the store of Duarte de León Jaramillo and the Royal Hospital for Indians. This youngest sister of Luis finally was burned at the stake on April 11, 1649, having suffered previously from cancer of the breast.

Leonor de Cáceres, niece of Luis de Carvajal, had lived with two different Catholic families at separate times over a period of four or five years, roughly between 1595 and 1600. After the imprisonment of her mother in 1595 she had first lived in the home of Agustín de Espindola, where a "blessed Negro," Anna de los Reyes, had taught her the fifteen mysteries of the rosary and other prayers. After her mother's execution in 1596 she was removed from this home by order of the Inquisition and placed with a second Catholic family, that of María de Peralta. Leonor had confessed twenty times and had received the sacrament of the Eucharist about seven times. However, it had not been possible to eradicate from her memory the prayers that she had been taught by her mother, her uncle Luis, and her aunts Isabel and Leonor, nor to control her secret observance of some Jewish practices. She had been conscious in her early life of a strong family attachment and the devotion of the members of the family to one another. Leonor had been the center of love and attention, since she was at that time the only offspring of the nine Carvajal children. Other than remembering having cried once that she was "dying of hunger" when the family insisted that she fast on Yom Kippur, the Great Day of the Lord, she had no unpleasant memories of family or Jewish life.

When she was called before the Inquisition, Leonor testified that she had been instructed that the Judaic law or law of Moses, also called the Hebraic law, had to be observed and that it was better than the laws of Christ. Her father, she said, had taught her the Our Father, the Hail Mary, the Creed, and the Hail Holy Queen, etc. She had heard her mother and father quarrel over his attempt to teach the child Catholic prayers. She had been taught that the true Messiah had not yet come. Leonor stated that she had begun to learn all these things from the time she was five years old.

She told the inquisitors that prior to 1595 her mother would spit many times after receiving the sacrament and leaving the church, but Leonor believed at the time of her testimony that the sacrament her mother had received was "truly God and a true man." She admitted that in her earlier years she had believed that the holy images were idols. She also stated that when she had gone to confession she had said only what her mother had told her to say.

The foregoing is a brief digest of the young girl's testimony given at four audiences in December 1600 to the same inquisitor, Alonso de Peralta, whose mien had made her uncle's flesh crawl with fear. In his questioning of Leonor one cannot detect anything but a conciliatory, suave approach. There was no attempt to trick her or threaten her. A partial explanation may be that Leonor could speak freely and fully. Those against whom she testified, with the exception of her father, were dead. They had been her teachers, and nothing she could say could injure them. Her testimony against her father, while unsparing, might be considered favorable on the whole, because he had taught her about Christianity and had been annoyed by his wife's Jewish practices. However, Leonor also testified that her father used to listen to Ruy Díaz Nieto and her uncle Luis discuss Judaism and that she once found her father reading Luis' little black prayer book.

From 1601 to 1650 Leonor led a more tranquil life than during her earlier years. About 1612, when she was approximately twenty-five, she married Lope Núñez, a muleteer. They had four children: Nicolas Núñez, born in 1614, who became a laborer; Ana María de León, born in 1618; Juan Núñez, born in 1622, who became a miner in Pachuca; and Antonio Díaz, born in 1626 and named after Leonor's father. Leonor's daughter, Ana María, married Manuel de la Rosa, a muleteer, and the couple had four children.

Leonor de Cáceres and Lope Núñez and their children lived for many years in Tulancingo, which is about ninety miles from Mexico City. Leonor's husband died about 1649. His wife continued to reside in peace in Tulancingo as she had done for almost forty years, until 1650, when the tranquility of her life came to an end. During the last few years before 1650 she served as a midwife and treated illnesses for the unemployed and other poor people.

Early in 1650 Leonor told her confessor that she had lied to the inquisitors during the proceedings against her in 1600. Her confessor instructed her that she was bound to reveal this to the Holy Office. The *fiscal*, prosecuting attorney for the Tribunal of the Holy Office, was in due course advised by Leonor of her prevarication and then filed charges against her on April 4, 1650. A copy of the charges was sent to her, and she was permitted to present an answer in writing before the representative of the Holy Office in Tulancingo. This she did on May 16, 1650. Her arrest was ordered on January 12, 1652, a year and a half later. She was taken into custody in her home town on January 24, 1652, at about 2:00 P.M. With the arresting officer she traveled for a day and a half to Mexico City. The officer had seized her bed and clothing and fifty pesos, all of which were carted to the Casa de la Inquisición.

Leonor had her first audience on February 1, 1652. At this time she gave her genealogy and some pertinent facts about her life. She stated that for almost four years, between 1596 and 1600, her aunt Mariana had resided with the same Catholic family to whom she, Leonor, had been entrusted. Leonor denied remembering her maternal grand-mother, but she did recall "having heard it said that a woman called Ana [Anica] de León, who was burned in the last auto-da-fé cele-brated in this city, was the sister of her mother, that her grandmother was called Francisca, and that she had been burned by the Inquisition."[9]

She recalled the names of all her aunts and uncles except Baltasar and Miguel. (They had escaped from Mexico when she was about four or five years old.) She stated that her uncle Fray Gaspar was now dead. She reported that her aunt Ana de León had married Cristóbal Miguel and that their daughter, María de León, had six children. The names of the children of María de León as stated by Leonor de Cáceres in her testimony vary from those found in the Mexican Inquisition Docu-ments. It is possible that María de León married more than once and that one listing of children is that of offspring from a marriage other than that to Diego Núñez.

Leonor further stated that she had known her cousin Ana, a daughter of María de León. This seemed to be the only one whom she knew personally. She did, however, know that Tomás, whom she named as another of María de León's children, had married in Mexico City; that, of the other children of this marriage, Catalina had married someone named Nieto; that the daughter named María had married a Rodrigo Núñez; Leonor had heard that this last-named couple had two or three children. The caliber of the morality of Leonor's father is revealed by her admission that she had a half-sister, a mulatta, Agustina de Quiñones, a "natural" daughter of her father.

Agustina had married Gaspar de Pastrana, a barber, but they had no

9. Mexican National Archives, Inquisition Section, Tomo 560 (1652), Expediente 21.

children. Leonor testified that she had stayed at the home of this half-sister after she had been permitted to remove her sanbenito. She had refused to go to her aunt Ana de León, or ever to see Fray Gaspar, because she "abhorred these people more than the devil, especially Doña Ana de León." As a seventeenth-century Catholic she might abhor association with her aunt who followed Jewish practices, but there is no explanation for her antagonism toward her uncle, a Dominican.

Leonor's statement about her aunt Ana explains why the paths of Anica and Leonor rarely crossed. In 1652 the secretary of the Inquisition noted that Leonor "recited very well" the Our Father, the Hail Mary, the Creed, the Hail Holy Queen, the Ten Commandments of God, the Commandments of the Church, the names of the sacraments, the Confiteor, and the Articles of Faith. She could read and write well, had read the medical book written by a Dr. Farfán, and had memorized some prescriptions so that she could treat the sick poor.

Leonor's recital of her life story to the Inquisition during her incarceration after 1652 contains many lacunae and some inconsistencies. She related that about 1608 her uncle Fray Gaspar had taken her from her home where she lodged to the house of her aunt Doña Ana. Leonor worked at her aunt's home for about a month. She stated that she and her aunt quarreled every day. There is no statement about the causes for the disputes. Finally Leonor left and went to live with her mulatta half-sister.

Leonor testified that after her marriage she went with her husband to Tulancingo, where she reared her family. She returned to Mexico City only twice between that time and her incarceration in the Inquisition cells. On one of these visits, about 1632, she stayed at the apartment of her aunt Ana de León. Leonor never explained why she went to her aunt's residence since she had parted from her in anger many years previously. She was not asked whether she had been in communication with her aunt during the intervening years.

After hearing the Edict of Faith[10] read in 1650, Leonor stated that she told her confessor that although she had fasted and observed the Sabbath for two years, she had not told this to the inquisitors in 1600. Her confessor had informed her that she must tell the Holy Office of

10. For a translation of the Edict, see Seymour B. Liebman, "The Long Night of the Inquisition," *Jewish Quarterly* (London), XIII (Summer, 1965), p. 28.

this dereliction, and she did so. In other, later testimony Leonor stated that this observance had been due to fear "as a crazy young girl" and that she had never since followed any Judaic observances.

In answer to the formal accusation during the 1652 proceedings Leonor recanted the testimony she had given fifty-two years earlier and labeled it "lies" which the devil had enticed her to state. She said that malevolent people, her "evil mother and her aunts Doña Ana de León and Doña Mariana had taught her the law of Moses" but that she had no recollection of having had anything to do with the law at that time. However, at another point during the testimony she admitted that she had observed Jewish practices during the period she had been in the home of Espindolas. At one hearing she fell to her knees and cried pitifully for mercy.

At the hearing of June 5, 1653, Leonor contradicted what she had said in 1652 and stated that all the testimony she had given in 1600 was true and that she should not have attempted to deny its veracity. On June 25, 1653, the inquisitors in executive session noted that she "appeared to be an old woman who might heed the suggestion of any demon," and consequently they ordered her release. It may be inferred that she suffered from senility, a condition that may give rise to fanaticism, inconsistencies, and misinterpretations.

The next entry in the Inquisition files pertinent to the Carvajal family is dated June 15, 1688, and refers to a petition of Bachiller (holder of a distinguished university degree) José Núñez, a cleric in minor orders. He was the son of Juan Núñez and Catalina de Salas and the grandson of Leonor de Cáceres, by this time deceased. Núñez asked for the testimony that his grandmother had given to the Holy Office. He aspired to become a priest and needed this testimony to "overcome the obstacle which was able to impede his promotion." For "legitimation of his person" he had to have proof that his grandmother had been acquitted in 1653. The three inquisitors unanimously denied his request on August 5, 1688, after reading all of Leonor's testimony. As far as the inquisitors were concerned, the taint of his great-great-grandmother Francisca de Carvajal had not been removed by the baptismal chrism that had been poured on the young cleric, on his mother and father, and on his grandmother Leonor, who had lived for more than fifty years as a good Catholic, performing deeds of charity to aid the sick and the poor.

The next and final entry in the Inquisition files concerning the descendants of the Carvajals is dated February 4, 1706, and is a petition of a great-grandson of Leonor de Cáceres, José de la Rosa, who resided at Tulancingo. He too wanted the testimony of Leonor de Cáceres, his great-grandmother, since one Miguel López, a neighbor, had made certain false charges against him, i.e., that he was not of "old Christians" and clean but was of "that evil race of the Jew, Moor, heretic, or others penanced by the Holy Office." José's grandmother was Ana de Cáceres, daughter of Leonor. Ana de Cáceres was the mother of two priests of the Mexico City archdiocese and of several other sons who had been admitted to Holy Orders, among them a Franciscan friar. All had been considered "clean of all bad races." José de la Rosa had to submit to the Holy Office the testimony of people who had known Leonor de Cáceres and could vouch that she had lived and died a good Catholic. A series of affidavits is affixed to the Inquisition files. From one of the affidavits we learn that José Núñez (wrongly called Juan in the affidavit) had become a priest without the testimony of the Inquisition records. We learn also that, after the death of her husband, Ana de Cáceres, daughter of Leonor, had been admitted to a religious order and had taken vows.

There were people still alive who could vouch for the integrity of Leonor de Cáceres. Several knew of her arrest in 1652 but recalled that she returned from Tulancingo without wearing the penitence habit required by the Inquisition when a person was being punished. The inquisitors ordered that a certificate be issued to José de la Rosa stating that Leonor de Cáceres had been reconciled in 1601 and that nothing incriminating had ever been found against her husband, Lope Núñez. The Inquisition noted that, in view of the issuance of the certificate, José de la Rosa did not at this time require the testimony that had been given by his great-grandmother Leonor. It was observed that if he did require it, the inquisitors would institute a new petition.

Interesting speculations arise about the possible descendants of Baltasar de Carvajal, brother of Luis, who escaped to Italy, changed his name to David Lumbroso, and of Miguel, who became Jacob Lumbroso. Jacob rose to fame as a physician and author in Venice and, for a time, was a rabbi in Salonica. In this regard attention is due to the researches of J. P. Hollander who wrote about a Dr. Jacob Lumbroso in an article entitled "Some Unpublished Material Relating to Dr.

Jacob Lumbrozo of Md." (see Bibliography) in which circumstantial evidence strongly suggests that this man may have been a Jew. Dr. Lumbroso was reported to have been in Maryland as early as 1658, and Mr. Hollander suggests that Italy was one of his early domiciles.

Mr. Hollander also indicated that as early as 1639 one Jacob Lumbroso flourished as a physician and rabbi in Venice. He was the author of a book *On Judaism* written in Spanish and a commentary on the Bible with a Spanish translation of some difficult portions of the sacred texts. Attempts have been made to establish a connection between the Italian and Maryland Lumbrosos.

It is possible that some members of this Lumbroso family were descendants of Baltasar or Miguel, who both adopted the patronymic of Lumbroso. It is certain that the surname Lumbroso was not a common one in Spain in an earlier era. Perhaps there may indeed be living Jewish descendants today of the family of Luis de Carvajal on the North American continent.

To the life and works of the young martyr Luis de Carvajal one can apply the words *Sic transit gloria mundi*. Luis and the inspiration he provided for his contemporaries were all but forgotten after *El Gran Auto de Fé* of April 11, 1649. His niece Leonor, to whom he had taught poetry and prayers, never mentioned his name during her hearings before the inquisitors in 1652 and 1653. If it were not for Vicente Riva Palacio, the likelihood exists that Luis might have been completely overlooked. Fortunately, Riva Palacio's *El Libro Rojo* (Mexico, 1867) inspired a painting of Isabel de Carvajal by David Alfero Siquerios and books by Pablo Martinez del Rio and others.

The tragic story of the members of the family known as Carvajal has received scant attention from historians despite the wealth of material it yields concerning many facets of Mexican history—material that can be mined from the procesos of the trials of the family members on file in the Mexican National Archives. The consuming flames of the Inquisition brought to an end some of those members of the primary family unit who remained in New Spain. The Spanish Church brought other branches of the family to an end through the vows of chastity taken by those who became secular priests or who joined monastic orders. Some branches of the family came to an end through natural causes. Others are unaccounted for and are not mentioned again in the Inquisition records. This would seem to imply that other survivors left the colony and found refuge abroad.

After 1763 the activities of the Holy Office against Jews decreased and became sporadic. The fame and luster of the name Carvajal diminished as new martyrs were made; and the name of Luis de Carvajal, *el Mozo*—Joseph Lumbroso, the Enlightened—was remembered no more.

Fig. 15: Several examples of sanbenitos (from an old Italian illustration)

selecteð Bibliography

Richard E. Greenleaf, in *Zummárraga and the Mexican Inquisition,* stated two basic premises for a study of the Mexican Inquisition. The first is that a detailed and thorough investigation of the trial records must be completed before valid generalizations can be drawn. The second premise and caveat is that many secondary sources are unreliable. Greenleaf mentions such renowned scholars as José Toribio Medina, Joaquín García Icazbalceta and Henry Charles Lea, as well as lesser known writers, whose works have some errors of translation, interpretation, or fact.

The Inquisition Section of the Mexican National Archives does not contain all the trial records. As part of the research supporting this work, I have read or studied documents at the Henry E. Huntington Library, the American Jewish Historical Society, the Henry C. Lea Memorial Library at the University of Pennsylvania, and a few manuscripts in the possession of private individuals. Professor Ivie E. Caidenhead graciously gave me his notes concerning Jews, from the trial records now at the Thomas E. Gilcrease Institute in Oklahoma. Because of the accuracy of the transcript, the records of Luis de Carvajal *el Mozo* printed by the Archivo General de la Nación were used in this study.

MANUSCRIPTS

All manuscripts are at the Mexican National Archives unless otherwise noted.

Proceso contra (Proceedings against) = P/c
por judaizante = pj
expediente (file number) = exp.

P/c Antón Carmona, por judío, Tomo 1A, exp. 2.

P/c Gonzalo Gómez, p/j, Tomo 2, exp. 2.

P/c Francisco Millan, por sospechoso de judaizante, Tomo 30, exp. 8.

P/c Juan Franco, Tomo 38, exp. 1. (Original charge was blasphemy but it was learned during the trial that he was a Jew.)

P/c Juan de Baeza, por sospechoso de judío, Tomo 125, exp. 4.

P/c Manuel Gómez Navarro, p/j, Tomo 151, exp. 6.

P/c Clara Enríquez, p/j (1595), Tomo 152, exp. 4.

P/c Justa Méndez, p/j (1595), Tomo 154, exp. 1. Also (1604) Tomo 1495, exp. 2.

P/c Diego Núñez Pacheco, p/j, Tomo 382, exp. 21.

P/c Isabel de Carvajal, p/j, Tomo 558, entire volume.

P/c Leonor de Cáceres, p/j (1652), Tomo 560, exp. 1. Also the proceso at the Henry E. Huntington Library, San Marino, California.

P/c José de la Rosa, (petition) Tomo 560, exp. 3.

P/c Luis de Carvajal, p/j, Tomo 1487, exp. 3. Second trial, judaizante relapso pertinaz, Tomo 1489, entire volume.

P/c Doña Francisca de Carvajal, p/j (1589), Tomo 1488, exp. 1. Also Tomo 223, exp. 2.

P/c Leonor de Andrade, p/j, Tomo 1488, exp. 2.

P/c Manuel Díaz, p/j, Tomo 1489, exp. 2.

P/c Antonio López de Morales, p/j (1595), Tomo 1490, exp. 1.

P/c Mariana de Carvajal, p/j, Tomo 1490, exp. 3.

Abecedario de los Relajados, Reconciliados, Penitenciados, in the Walter Douglas Collection, Henry E. Huntington Library, San Marino, California.

PUBLISHED MATERIAL

The Holy Bible in various editions including the Douay, Vulgate, Jewish Publication Society translation, and the Authorized Version as used by Chief Rabbi J. H. Hertz in *The Pentateuch and Haftorahs*, London, 1936.

Anales del Museo Nacional de Arqueología. "Ultimos momentos y conversión de Luis de Carvajal, 1596." No author. Vol. III (1925), pp. 64–78.

Baron, Salo Wittmayer. *History and Jewish Historians.* Philadelphia: Jewish Publication Society, 1964.

Becker, Carl L. *The Heavenly City of the Eighteenth Century Philosophers.* New Haven: Yale University Press, 1932.

Benítez, Fernando. *La vida criolla en el siglo XVI.* Mexico City: Ediciones Era, 1953.

Bocanegra, P. Mathias. *Relación Auto General de Fée celebrado . . . 11 de abril, 1649.* Mexico: Holy Office, 1649.

Carreño, Alberto María. "Luis de Carvajal, el Mozo," *Memorias de la Academia de Historia,* XV (Jan.–March, 1956), pp. 87–101.

Díaz, Bernal del Castillo. *Historia verdadera de la conquista de la Nueva España.* Mexico City: Editorial Porrua, 1960.

García, Genaro. *Documentos inéditos o muy raros para la historia de México.* 28 vols. Mexico City: Libreria de la Viuda de Ch. Bouret, 1904–1910.

García, Joaquín Icazbalceta. *Bibliografía mexicana del siglo XVI.* Mexico City: Fondo de Cultura Económica, 1954.

Greenleaf, Richard E. *Zumárraga and the Mexican Inquisition.* Washington, D.C.: Academy of American Franciscan History, 1961.

Gumbiner, Joseph. "The Indian Jews of Mexico," *American Judaism,* V (Jan., 1956), pp. 11–14.

Haring, Clarence H. *The Spanish Empire in America.* New York: Harcourt, Brace & World, 1947.

Hollander, J. P. "Some Unpublished Material Relating to Dr. Jacob Lumbrozo of Md.," *Publications of the American Jewish Historical Society,* I (1893), p. 25.

Lea, Henry Charles. *The Inquisition in the Spanish Dependencies.* New York: The Macmillan Co., 1922.

Libro Primero de Votos de la Inquisición de México. Mexico City: Archivo General de la Nación, 1949.

Liebman, Seymour B. "The Abecedario and a Check-List of Mexican Inquisition Documents in the Henry E. Huntington Library," *Hispanic American Historical Review,* LXIV (1964), pp. 554–567.

Liebman, Seymour B. *Guide to Jewish References in the Mexican Colonial Era.* Philadelphia: Univ. of Pennsylvania Press, 1964.

Liebman, Seymour B. "Hernando Alonso: The First Jew on the North American Continent," *Journal of Inter-American Studies,* V (1963), pp. 291–296.

Liebman, Seymour B. "The Long Night of the Inquisition," *Jewish Quarterly* (London), XIII (Summer, 1965), pp. 28–33.

Liebman, Seymour B. "Mexican Mestizo Jews," *American Jewish Archives,* XIX (November, 1967), pp. 144–174.

Marcus, Jacob R. (No title.) *American Jewish Archives,* XVII (April, 1965), p. 17.

Martinez del Río, Pablo. *"Alumbrado."* Mexico City: Porrua Hermanos, 1937.

Medina, José Toribio. *El Tribunal del Santo Oficio de la Inquisición en México.* Mexico City: Libreria Navarro, 1954.

Pallares, Eduardo. *El Procedimiento Inquisitorial.* Mexico City: Imprinta Universitaria, 1951.

Patai, Raphael. "Venta Prieta Revisited," *Midstream,* XI (March, 1965), pp. 79–92.

Procesos de Luis de Carvajal, el Mozo. Mexico City: Archivo General de la Nación, 1935.

Ricard, Robert. "Pour une étude du Judaisme portugais au Mexico," *Revue d'Histoire Moderne,* XIV (1939), pp. 519–526.

Riva, Vincente Palacio (ed.). *México a traves de los siglos.* 5 vols. Mexico: Publicaciones Herrerias, no date.

Roth, Cecil. *A History of the Marranos.* New York & Philadelphia: Jewish Publication Society & World, 1959.

Tibon, Gutierre. *Un País en Futuro.* Mexico City: Editorial Pirámide, 1950.

Toro, Alfonso. *La Familia Carvajal.* 2 vols. Mexico City: Editorial Patria, 1944.

Toro, Alfonso. *Los Judíos en la Nueva España.* Mexico City: Archivo General de la Nación, 1932. (Material collated from Tomo 77 of the Ramo de la Inquisición.)

Vásquez de Espinosa, Antonio. *La Nueva España en el siglo XVI.* Mexico City: Editorial Patria, 1944.

index

A NOTE ABOUT THIS EDITION OF

THE ENLIGHTENED

*This book was designed by Harvey Satenstein of New York,
and set by American Book–Stratford Press of NYC.
The body type face is 11 on 12 point Linotype Granjon,
and the display type 24 and 36 point Libra
(similar to volumes of the period by Master Printer Juan Pablos,
the first printer in the New World).
The entire book was printed in offset lithography by
Polygraphic Company of America, Inc., North Bennington, Vt.
The text stock is 60 lb. Weyerhaeuser's Scholar Antique Laid,
and the cover material a specially-made Monk's cloth
manufactured by Wall Fabrics, Inc. of Paterson, N.J.
that simulates the color and texture of the burlap sanbenito
worn by penitents. Black Canco endpapers and
black top stain are reminders of this dark period of history.
Green-and-white headbands show the colors of the
official seal of the Inquisition in Mexico.
The stamping is in sanguine colored leaf,
and the onlay on the cover of the binding was printed by
offset lithography, by Clarke & Way, Inc., NYC.
The binding work was executed by The Book Press Incorporated
of Brattleboro, Vt. The jacket was printed by
Martin Lithographers, Inc., NYC.
on 70 lb. Weyerhaeuser's Hamilton Kilmory Chestnut Laid*